101
WAYS TO
ADVERTISE
YOUR BUSINESS

ALSO BY ANDREW GRIFFITHS

101 Ways to Market Your Business
101 Survival Tips for Your Business
101 Ways to Really Satisfy Your Customers

101

WAYS TO ADVERTISE YOUR BUSINESS

ANDREW GRIFFITHS

ALLEN&UNWIN

This book aims to provide general ideas and information about running a small business. It is produced without assuming responsibility and is sold with the understanding that the publisher and the author are not engaged in providing professional advice to the reader. This book is not intended to supersede independent professional advice.

Neither author nor publisher take any responsibility for loss occasioned to any person or organisation acting or refraining from action as a result of information contained in this publication.

First published in 2004

Allen & Unwin
83 Alexander Street
Crows Nest NSW 2065
Australia
Phone: (61 2) 8425 0100
Fax: (61 2) 9906 2218
Email: info@allenandunwin.com
Web: www.allenandunwin.com

National Library of Australia
Cataloguing-in-Publication entry:

Griffiths, Andrew, 1966– .
101 ways to advertise your business: building a successful
business with smart advertising.

ISBN 1 86508 982 6.

1. Advertising. I. Title.

659.1

Set in 12/14 pt Adobe Garamond by Midland Typesetters, Maryborough, Victoria
Printed by Griffin Press, South Australia

10 9 8 7 6 5 4 3 2 1

Contents

Acknowledgments

As I sit and ponder how I came to write this book my thoughts go to the individuals and businesses who let me loose on their advertising. I am glad to report they are all still in business and doing very well. In particular, I would like to thank the following people for their faith in me: Peter and Lynne Strangman, Neville Burman, John Hill and Liz Shuter, David Robertson, Sean Ffinch, Tom Stevens, Stephen O'Reilly, Jane Baxter and last but by no means least, the entire team from Beaches Health Studio.

There are also a number of people, who have been a constant source of support to me as a writer. I would like to thank Robert Reid, my literary role model, mentor and all-round good bloke, and my publishers at Allen & Unwin who have been incredibly loyal and supportive. In return I constantly supply their Sydney office with confectionary and as we have more books in this series to produce, I would suggest the entire team join Weight Watchers immediately!

In my own office I would like to issue a special thank you to Sandra, Natalie and Susan—each of you provides me with a much valued source of support and entertainment. Not too many hours go by without some serious belly laughter in our office and for that I thank you.

I would also like to thank my mother-in-law (yes that's right) for making me part of a very memorable and wonderful family. I went from having virtually no relatives to about a million overnight—an advertising success story if ever there was one.

And last, but not least, Carolyne, who really is the advertising guru in this relationship.

Introduction

101 Ways to Advertise Your Business is written for anyone who wants to attract more customers. Today there are a multitude of advertising options available and it is often hard to decide where to advertise, let alone how to make your advertising effective. This book will benefit anyone who has to make any decisions about advertising their services or products. This might include business owners and managers, marketing managers, students and even advertising and marketing consultants.

Many people complain that business books offer advice that is too difficult, too expensive or too time consuming to apply to their own business. The concept of the books in the 101 series is to provide simple and reliable business advice from people with a strong background in small business. This gives the books a very practical advantage over other similar publications. The 101 series takes into consideration the three most common small business restrictions to implementing new ideas and concepts to build the business: lack of time; lack of money; and lack of simple 'how to' instructions to implement the advice given. *101 Ways to Advertise Your Business* will prove especially helpful in the following situations:

1. when you are planning your advertising activities for the coming year

2. when you are weighing up different advertising options and deciding how to best spend your dollars
3. when you are developing your advertisement or commercial
4. when you are negotiating prices for buying advertising.

Like all of the books written in the 101 series, *101 Ways to Advertise Your Business* provides a wealth of information in a simple format, giving practical advice aimed at increasing the results from all your advertising. It will enable you to make informed decisions about where to advertise, how much to spend on advertising and how to make your advertisements produce better results.

What's in this book

The first section of this book covers information relating to advertising in general; what it is, how it works, when it goes wrong, and how much to spend on your campaigns. Sections 2 to 11 contain the 101 tips which are simple, easy to implement ideas and strategies that will definitely help your business. The tips are divided into the following categories:

Advertising in newspapers
Making television advertising work for you
Have some fun on radio
Telephone directories—important for all businesses
High-impact outdoor signage
Direct mail advertising
Advertising in magazines
Advertising with other businesses
Writing your advertisement—the copy is critical
Using the Internet to advertise your business

There is also a Bonus Section with 20 additional advertising tips.

One of the biggest stumbling blocks for many people planning advertising is what words and phrases to use. The advertising industry is filled with jargon that the average person would have no chance of understanding (and to be honest I think half the people in the advertising industry aren't really sure what most of this jargon means!). If you want to learn some of the lingo then the glossary at the back of the book is for you. Remember though, that if someone is throwing jargon at you and you don't know what it means, ask them. It is important that before committing to advertising in any shape or format, you are completely aware of what you are getting for your money.

I have also included a chapter called 'Smart advertising words and phrases'. This is a quick reference guide designed to help you find the right kinds of words and phrases to give your advertisements extra punch.

The blank forms provide tools to help you develop customised advertising checklists. These will increase the quality of your advertising and ensure that advertisements produced are as effective as possible.

At the end of the book I have also included a list of books that I consider well worth reading, especially if you want to increase the effectiveness of your advertising and marketing as a whole. Developing a library of reference books proves beneficial to any business owner and now, more than ever, there are some excellent books available. Put them on your Christmas or birthday lists or commit to buying a new book once a month—before you know it you will have a very good collection of ideas and suggestions for building your business.

As with all good advice, the most important messages are often the most simple. For this reason several important messages and themes are repeated throughout this book. The aim is to give you a clear understanding of the factors that will make your advertising work better and ultimately attract more customers to your business.

All of the books in the 101 series are written in a style that appeals to those who like to read a book from cover to cover, as well as those who like to open a book at any page to search for an idea or a suggestion that will be relevant to their business right at this moment. I strongly suggest you keep this book handy and use it as a source of constant reference and inspiration. The ideas won't date and the tips and recommendations can be used in virtually any business.

1 | Getting a handle on advertising

What is advertising? This is of course the logical question to ask. The word is thrown around a lot, often in the same sentence as marketing and selling. My definitions for these terms are as follows:

- **Marketing:** Essentially, marketing is the process used to build a business. There are many tools within the process including advertising, selling, customer service and market research.
- **Advertising:** Specifically, advertising is used to attract customers to a business. This may mean physically getting them to a business, or picking up a telephone or visiting a website.
- **Selling:** Once advertising has been used to attract the customer to the business the selling process takes over and the appropriate skills and facilities are utilised to sell a product or service to the customer.

At some stage in the evolution of any business, the owners will need to address the issue of advertising, and when they do, they will be confronted with a myriad of options that can be confusing and complicated. Where should you advertise and why? How do you advertise? And how do you make an advertisement?

Recently I was discussing the option of advertising on television with a client of mine who runs a restaurant. I was busily explaining what we would do, how it would work and how wonderful it would be when he stopped me and asked, 'How do you make a television commercial?' I immediately launched into the usual 'You don't have to worry about that as we do it all' response. He stopped me again and said, 'That's not what I mean. I want to know how you physically make a television commercial from start to finish because I have absolutely no idea where to even start'.

This made me stop and think. For most people in business this is a very honest and fair question. Making an advertisement is second nature for people in the advertising industry but for the average business owner it is like learning a foreign language.

This book will address all the questions you might have about any type of advertising and I hope that after reading it you will feel ready to take on the advertising world to build your business. Don't be afraid to ask questions like my client did—who, by the way, became actively involved in the making of his television commercial, which has gone on to produce major success for the business.

Does advertising really work?

This is a question I get asked all the time, usually by people who are sceptical about the benefits of advertising. I have to say unequivocally that yes, advertising does work but it is not an exact science and, more often than not, it is a matter of trial and error. Now I know this does not inspire a lot of confidence in the advertising process; however, like all forms of promoting a business, the more information you have and the more time and energy you put into your advertising, the greater the results will be.

From my own experience I see a lot of businesses that simply dabble in the field of advertising. After running one newspaper advertisement that doesn't produce the expected results they make sweeping statements like 'newspaper advertising doesn't work'. Of course newspaper advertising *does* work but it depends on a number of factors. For example, what is the advertisement like, where is it placed in the newspaper, what is the product or service being promoted and what are the other outside influences that could affect the results. More often than not, businesses don't really have good monitoring systems in place to determine where new customers are coming from, making it virtually impossible to determine if an advertisement has worked or not.

Another common problem with advertising is that many business owners have unrealistic expectations about the returns from their advertising. For a couple of hundred dollars they expect the advertising to return tens of thousands of dollars. This just doesn't happen. If it was that easy every small business owner would be a multimillionaire.

I have been involved in a lot of businesses that have started their advertising with some trepidation. I have watched them slowly build their businesses with smart and effective advertising to the point where they have grown into large corporations that spend hundreds of thousands of dollars per year on advertising.

So in response to the question, 'Does advertising really work?', the answer is yes, it most certainly does, but the key is how you advertise and where you advertise.

The five most important things you need to know about successful advertising

So what is it that makes a successful advertisement effective? There are five key areas that I believe are the very essence of effective advertising. They are:

1. establishing the exact message you are trying to put forward
2. being clear about your target audience
3. making your advertisement stand out from millions of others
4. ensuring people see your advertising often
5. giving your advertising time to work.

Each of these areas are explained in more detail below.

1. Establishing the exact message you are trying to put forward

A lot of advertising sends a very confusing message to potential customers. Advertising needs to be planned and it needs to be simple. Sit down and allow some time to think about the exact message you are trying to pass on to potential customers. Give them a reason to pick up the telephone or to drop into your business.

Often advertising becomes cluttered and confusing because there is simply too much information in the advertisement or commercial. If you can't summarise what you want your message to say in one short sentence, go back to the drawing board until you can. Once this magic sentence has been determined, build your advertisement to portray this message clearly. Your advertising will have far greater results if you repeat this message rather than try to introduce a number of other messages.

Take a few minutes to flick through today's newspaper and pay close attention to the advertisements that really stand out. They are often the least cluttered. They will have a clear message. They may promote a lot of products but there is no doubt about what they are selling and what the message they are trying to get across is.

For advertising to work for any business, deciding the specific message you want to pass on to potential customers is critical.

2. Being clear about your target audience

If you are advertising parachuting courses it is unlikely you will get the best results from a commercial on television during daytime soap operas (apart from some adventurous retirees perhaps). Likewise, if you are selling a new product to relieve the pain of arthritis it is unlikely to produce excellent results if it is advertised during coverage of some world extreme sport (although many participants will definitely need the product in a few years).

Knowing exactly the type of person you want to see your advertisement is an essential component for planning your campaign. This is a question most advertising sales representatives will normally ask you (or at least they should ask you). The advertising lingo for it is the 'demographic' you are trying to reach. This can include such details as the age of the potential customers, their sex, their wealth status and their geographical location, to mention a few of the elements of a demographic breakdown.

Advertising should be planned to reach particular kinds of consumers in a specific manner. The clearer you are about your targeted customers the more effectively you can plan your advertising. Placing advertisements randomly in any medium is not an effective way to advertise. Different people watch television at different times (and of course they watch different shows). Different people read various sections of the paper, listen to particular radio stations and so on.

Whenever you are planning an advertising campaign take a few moments to stop and consider the exact type of person you want to see your advertisements.

3. Making your advertisement stand out from millions of others

The main reason advertising doesn't work for a lot of businesses is because the advertisement or commercial fails to catch the attention of the targeted customers. It is very important to remember that consumers are bombarded with advertising from the minute they wake up until the minute they go to bed. Some statistics have noted that on average we can be exposed to over 30 000 advertising messages a day. This may sound ridiculous, but think about what you are exposed to during your typical day.

You are woken by a radio alarm and the station you are listening to is the start of the day's selling process. As you shower and get ready for work a multitude of products fight for your attention. Then you might sit down to watch the morning news while having some breakfast and you are bombarded by the advertisements on the television as well as on the products you have for breakfast, such as the cereal box. If you read the paper in the morning you are also going to be exposed to hundreds, if not thousands of advertising messages. Then it's time to go to work and in the car you might listen to the radio, which exposes you to the obligatory radio commercials. During a 30-minute drive it is likely you will see thousands of signs along the roadside advertising businesses. If you travel by public transport there are signs inside the trains and buses. Once you are at work and you check your mail you see even more advertising. Check your email and there is advertising. By now it is about 9 a.m., you have been up for only a couple of hours and you have already seen thousands of advertisements.

It is easy to see why it is important your advertising stands out from the crowd.

4. Ensuring people see your advertising often
'Frequency' is the advertising lingo used to describe how often an advertisement will appear and, as a result, how often people will see it. This is really the most simple aspect of advertising—get as many people as possible to see your advertisement as often as possible and your advertising will bring much greater results.

The downside to this is that the more frequency you want for your advertising the more it will cost. A simple example of this is that of television advertising. To air a commercial at 3 a.m., a time when few people are watching television, will cost a fraction of a commercial aired during the nightly news (generally the most viewed program).

The aim is to look at your whole campaign and make certain you are going to reach as many people as often as possible. Advertising in more than one area is a key to this, so it is wise to consider this strategy. We always recommend to our clients that they consider at least two mediums, such as television and radio, or radio and newspaper for their campaigns.

5. Giving your advertising time to work

An interesting phenomenon of advertising is that you have to give your advertising time to work. It is very rare for a potential customer to see your advertisement once, then race off to pick up the phone or jump in the car. It takes seeing an advertisement a number of times (often in a number of different places) before consumers are convinced they need your product or service. One example of this is selling through Internet sites.

It will generally take a person seven visits to a website before they will make a specific purchase. Each of these visits will have a different reason behind the visit, most occurring subconsciously, but they are all equally important visits and most of the time they are to do with establishing the credibility of the company the customer is looking to make the purchase from. So placing one advertisement and expecting to be inundated with responses is generally not realistic.

On the upside, though, the response to an advertisement will generally increase the longer it is out there because more people will see the advertising more often. I have monitored a lot of advertising campaigns where we have done the same amount of advertising for a specific product over a six-month period. Each month the response increased, with the last month being the most successful, illustrating the long-term benefits of advertising. Likewise it takes a while for advertising to stop working once the momentum is gained. For those campaigns we ran for six months and then stopped, new customers continued to flow for up to two months before finally slowing to a trickle or stopping. Hence, I often hear business owners say that when they stopped advertising there was no impact on the number of new customers for the business. A few months later, however, they often come back saying that new customers have dried up and they need to start advertising again (and quickly).

I like to use the analogy that advertising is similar to pushing a broken-down car (something most of us have had the joy of experiencing). Getting the car moving is tough, but once it is moving it takes less energy to keep it going. If you stop pushing the car it will take a while to stop as it moves under its own momentum (see the 'Old bomb principle' in tip #19).

Where does advertising go wrong?

Most of the points listed below are the opposite of the five key elements of advertising success I spoke about above. By understanding the most common advertising mistakes you will be able to devise strong focus for your advertising needs. Advertisements and commercials go wrong mostly because they:

1. are done on impulse, i.e. not enough time is spent planning the advertising
2. are aimed at the wrong people
3. are cluttered and confusing
4. feature in the wrong medium

5. feature in only one advertising medium
6. are seen at the wrong time
7. don't stand out from the crowd
8. don't give the customer a reason to act immediately
9. don't make the product or service appealing enough to interest the consumer
10. are stopped before the advertising can work, that is, a lack of repeat advertising.

All of the above are discussed throughout this book and, without hesitation, I believe most advertising has at least three or four of the above errors.

How do you know if your advertising works?

There is an old saying in the advertising industry, 50 per cent of advertising works and 50 per cent doesn't—the real key is to identify which half is which. Most advertising is assessed by general feelings such as, 'I don't think it really worked', or, 'It worked a bit', or, 'I am not really sure if it worked or not'. Surely anyone who spends one dollar on advertising would want to know whether or not it works and, most importantly, how well it worked? All advertising needs to be monitored and assessed on a regular basis to see how well it is working and there are a number of ways to do this.

The most simple method is to monitor sales of the particular product or service you are promoting. If sales go up when you advertise it is reasonable to assume your advertising works. If sales don't go up (assuming you have given the advertising time to work) then your advertising probably isn't working and you may need to revisit your campaign.

Another method I strongly recommend is a simple questionnaire for customers. This can be placed at the front of any business (i.e. at the reception), allowing staff to ask customers how they heard about the business. The form can be a flick-and-tick format, where the staff member ticks the appropriate box. Alternatively, most modern-day cash registers can be programmed to collect this information and reports can be prepared accordingly. Asking this question over the telephone is also an option.

I encourage all of my clients to make certain they ask new customers where they heard about the business. Customers are usually more than happy to answer this question, regardless of the manner you use to collect the information. The key is to make sure you do collect the information so you can use it to plan future advertising. The information can be reviewed, say once a week or month, and it gives a good indication of what advertisements are being seen.

There is a blank form at the back of this book (see page 235) that can be used to form your own advertising results checklist.

How much should you spend on advertising?

This is probably the most common question I am asked and it is a good question. Over the years I have read facts, figures and opinions on what businesses should spend on marketing, which incorporates advertising and promotional material. Personally I don't think there is a black and white figure that should be quoted. It really depends on a number of issues.

The easiest way to summarise what your advertising expenditure needs to be relates to how much new business you want. If you have a business that is in a growth stage, then advertise more. If you are in a business that can handle a lot more customers with minimal operational changes, advertise more. If you are trying to consolidate your business after a particular growth spurt, advertise less. My own ball-park figure recommendations are: for businesses in growth stages spend 10 per cent of your turnover, and for those in a consolidation stage spend about 5 per cent.

Regardless of how much you spend, make certain you

budget for this activity to be an ongoing expense, not just something done when there is a little extra cash in the bank account. If you feel you can't afford to advertise perhaps it is worth looking at the prices you charge. Advertising is a normal business expense and it should be included when you are planning your yearly budgets.

Sadly a lot of businesses only advertise when they are desperate for new customers and that puts them under a lot of pressure to get results. Businesses that advertise regularly tend to get the best and most consistent results. A problem that can arise from spasmodic advertising is a sudden, large influx of new customers, which the business then struggles to accommodate. This can actually lead to losing customers because the level of customer service drops, delays are encountered and staff become stressed.

The constantly changing face of advertising

Advertising is a constantly changing business. Everyday there are new places to advertise and lots of people and companies trying to convince you to spend your advertising dollar with them. There was a time when there was one newspaper, a couple of television and radio stations and perhaps the odd roadside billboard. Now, where do you start?

This is the nature of the advertising business. It is dynamic and constantly evolving with new ways to advertise being invented daily. Often this can be a little overwhelming for the average business owner. I suggest you take some time to listen to new advertising sales pitches and be prepared to try new advertising mediums, but always adhere to the guidelines provided in this book.

Remember also, every advertising sales representative walking through the door will tell you they have the very best product available. They can't all be the best but often you will come across one that is perfect for your business and it is affordable. If you want independent advice use a marketing or advertising consultant as they are able to offer impartial advice on where to spend your advertising dollar so it works the best.

The main point to be gained from this section is to keep an open mind to advertising. In coming years there will be even more avenues for advertising and smart business owners will take the time to look at all of their options before making any commitments.

2 | Advertising in newspapers

The printed advertisement has been around for a long time and newspapers go back almost 200 years. Today they are still one of the main media for businesses to advertise their products and services and, like all advertising venues, there are many potential pitfalls for the unwary advertiser.

I am a big believer in the benefits of newspaper advertising, however a large proportion of newspaper advertisements are ineffectual and, as a result, they would bring limited business to the organisations they are promoting. In this section I discuss the key issues to consider when planning newspaper advertisements. By following these recommendations you will be able to increase the effectiveness of your advertising and ultimately attract more business.

I suggest that whenever you are planning newspaper advertising you read through this section to make certain you have addressed the key issues to ensure your newspaper advertising works effectively. The issues covered here are:

#1   Decide what message you are trying to send
#2   Keep your advertisement simple, uncluttered and easy to read
#3   Make your advertisement stand out
#4   Placement is critical

1 Decide what message you are trying to send

When planning any newspaper advertising it is essential you put some serious thought into exactly what message you are trying to send to readers. All too often business owners deliberate over where to place an advertisement, how big it should be, whether to use colour or black and white, and what day they should place the advertisement in the newspaper. All of these issues are important and they are addressed in the following pages but, without a doubt, deciding on the right message is by far the most important part of an advertisement.

The message includes issues such as what are the products or services you want to sell or promote, why should customers buy your products or services, when should they buy them and how they can buy them. This is the who, what, when and how of developing an advertisement. The questions that need to be asked are:

1. **Exactly what do you want to achieve from the advertisement?**
   This is really the goals and objectives of your advertisement. This can be translated into financial goals and objectives of the advertisement or, in simple terms, how much business you would like to receive from the advertisement. As discussed in the preliminary section of this book it is very hard to know what the exact results will be from an advertisement but as a minimum it is fair to assume you will want to recoup your advertising costs. The more advertising you do the better you will become at forecasting results. Setting unrealistic goals only leads to disappointment and loss of confidence in the advertising medium you have chosen.

2. **Why should customers buy the product or service you are advertising?**
   It is important you tell readers why the product or service you are advertising is worth purchasing. This may include

reasons such as a special price, a new product, limited availability or a combination of the above.

3. **When should customers buy the product or service you
are advertising?**
If you want customers to buy your product today, tell them
so. If you are advertising a special happening over a one-
month period, advertise that. Decide when you want customers to buy your product or service and tell them in the
advertisement.

4. **How can they buy the product or service you are
advertising?**
Let customers know exactly how they can buy the product
or service you are advertising. For example, do they have to
come to your business or can they buy it over the telephone
or Internet? Spell this out clearly and you will achieve greater
results.

As you can see, there are important questions to be asked before
even starting the design of the advertisement or thinking about
where you would like to place it in the newspaper. You will
greatly increase your chances of achieving good results with
your newspaper advertising if you take some time to sit down
and address the above issues first.

2 Keep your advertisement simple, uncluttered and easy to read

Just take a quick flick through any newspaper and you'll find some really good advertisements, and some shockers. The most common mistake with many newspaper advertisements is that they are cluttered with far too much information, confusing the message. Generally such a mass of information makes it virtually impossible to notice the advertisement, let alone take the time to try and figure it out.

I always suggest to anyone who is planning to advertise in newspapers that they start a file (or use a shoe box) for advertisements that have caught their eye. This includes some from those newspapers you don't normally read. Visit the local newsagents and buy a few international newspapers or even foreign language papers—I love doing this with foreign papers because I can't understand a word in the advertisement so I have to rely totally on what grabs my attention. I keep a pile of scrapbooks that have all types of advertisements in them, promoting everything from bras to bazookas (yes bazookas!) as the subject matter is almost irrelevant. The layout is what's critical.

The most attention grabbing advertisements tend to have bold headings with lots of white space around them. They are uncluttered, easy to read and the messages are simple. They follow the format of who, what, when and how and they make it easy for the reader to quickly glance at the advertisement and make some kind of decision on the spot. That decision may be to get in the car and rush straight to the business to buy the product or it may be to file the information into the memory banks for later, when the customer wants to purchase a product or service like the one advertised.

Often people feel that too much white space in an advertisement is like throwing money away. When paying by the centimetre (or inch) they feel they have to pack as much into the advertisement as possible to get value for their advertising dollar. All they are doing is reducing the effectiveness of the advertisement, therefore they are wasting money.

Another common fault with printed advertisements is the use of too many different styles of fonts or type. An advertisement should really only have two or three different fonts—maximum. Lots of fonts makes an advertisement hard to read and it gives the appearance of being amateurish. Look at the best advertisements produced by the leading companies worldwide and you will see that generally the number of fonts used is kept to a minimum. Script fonts (fonts designed to be like handwriting) are also often hard to read and as a result they can be overlooked. Of course there are exceptions to this rule (Coca-Cola is one) but generally script fonts are used to promote a brand rather than a particular product or service.

Once you have decided on the key messages you want your advertisement to pass on, start planning the look and layout of your advertisement, keeping in mind the issues discussed in this tip.

3 Make your advertisement stand out

If your advertisement doesn't stand out, the effectiveness is dramatically reduced and so are the end results. Many newspaper readers just scan their daily paper. Because of this you only have a few seconds to make your advertisement catch the reader's attention.

I am a big advocate of bold headings and questions in printed advertisements. If you ask a question the reader will attempt to answer it. Questions stand out and they draw a reader's eye to the advertisement. Likewise there are many words that can be used to draw attention to an advertisement. At the back of this book I have included a section of words that attract attention in advertisements (see page 214). These can be adapted to suit your business and the products or services you are selling.

All too often modern design and trendy looks overshadow the desired end result of an effective advertisement. While I am a lover of quality graphic design it is important not to lose sight of the objective of the advertisement, which will generally be to sell something. Whenever you are planning a newspaper advertisement I suggest getting your designer or newspaper to give you a copy of the advertisement so you can put it on a page in a newspaper to see how well it stands out. The paper your advertisement will be printed on is probably better than the quality of the newspaper you will be comparing it against but you will still be able to get a feeling for how the advertisement will look in the final product. This is an excellent way to determine if your advertisement is likely to catch attention or simply blend in with the other information on the page, generally meaning that it will not work.

4 Placement is critical

Deciding where to place your advertisement in any newspaper is often a tough decision. Newspapers are divided in sections and it is normal to pay more for prime locations. Some of the most popular places (and this generally means the parts of the newspaper that are read by the most people) will cost more than other areas.

Early in the newspaper (called early general news) is considered a prime location. This encompasses the first 25 per cent of the newspaper and it is where most of the core news stories are located. Advertising in this section is the most expensive, with page 3 (the first right-hand page after the cover) being considered the best. To advertise on an early page there is normally a loading or surcharge on top of the normal advertising rate.

Right-hand pages are also considered premium locations. The earlier the right-hand page the more desirable and as a result the more expensive the advertising space will be. There are some arguments about the reality of whether people are more likely to read right-hand pages or not. I can only talk from my own experience and I have to say we have had the best results for clients with advertising on the early right-hand pages. While we pay a premium, the advertisements are read by more people.

There are a lot of other sections in the newspaper considered premium locations and most of these are never short of advertisers. Each newspaper is slightly different and this information will be supplied to you by advertising sales representatives of the newspapers you are interested in.

Like all advertising the real key is to have as many people as possible see your advertisement, so keep this in mind when planning your campaign.

5 Black and white, colour or spot colour?

Most newspapers offer advertising in black and white (mono), full colour or spot colour. The cheapest advertisements are normally black and white, then spot colour, with full colour the most expensive. There are advantages and disadvantages with each.

Mono advertisements work well, readers are used to them, but it can be somewhat difficult to make an advertisement on a whole page of black and white type stand out. An advantage of black and white advertisements, though, is that you can be very specific about where you want the advertisement to appear, right down to the exact page number.

Spot colour means using one particular colour in your advertisement. The colour you can use generally depends on the newspaper and any other advertisements they are running at the time. The way newspapers are printed means that two and sometimes four pages are printed together. They are not corresponding pages—1, 2, 3 and 4—but generally a section. They may be pages 3, 4, 31 and 32, depending on how many pages there are in the paper. This means that if you want to use spot colour you often have to forfeit exact position or page number for the privilege. You will also pay a premium. The upside is that it can really make an advertisement stand out.

The most common spot colours used are red and blue. Magenta (reddish purple) also really stands out well but a lot of papers don't use this colour. If using spot colour, take some time to think about how to make it work for you. Too much use of the spot colour and the advertisement becomes a mess. It is generally better to use it as an attention grabbing device, such as a big price, a bold statement, a strong colour board, for branding or something similar. Again, I recommend looking through various newspapers to find examples that use spot colour to really make the advertisement stand out. See how they have used the colour to catch your attention.

Finally there is full colour. This can be very effective—however, there are a number of downsides. First and foremost is the expense. Full colour comes at a price and generally it is quite a lot more than the other options (I have seen it double the price). Secondly, most newspaper printing is reasonably low quality and as a result the reproduction can be quite poor. The paper used is the cheapest available, which is pretty reasonable for a product with a shelf life of perhaps one or two days before it is used to wrap vegetable peels, so full colour advertisements can be a little flat in appearance. Sometimes they can be a little blurry. In all fairness the printing presses, papers and inks being used are getting better but they are nowhere near the quality of glossy magazines. Advertisers are therefore often disappointed with their full-colour newspaper advertisements because they had unrealistic expectations of the quality. Have a look through your bundle of newspapers and see the quality for yourself. Full-colour advertisements can be used very well in newspapers but the advertisement needs to be well designed and the fact that the printing process is not as sharp as laser printers or glossy magazines needs to be taken into consideration.

Use colour to draw attention to the advertisement rather than highlight what is in the advertisement. Make your advertisements less complex colour wise and don't clutter the advertisement.

6 Different people read different parts of the newspaper

When thinking about where to place your advertisement keep in mind that different people will read different parts of the paper. I know that in my household I tend to read the general news first, then the business pages, the cartoons and the classifieds. My wife goes straight for the entertainment pages, special features and the movie guide. Some people will flip straight to the sports section and others to the television page, which they may read repeatedly while they watch television. For this reason it is important to think about where you want your advertisement to appear.

Think about the type of people you want to read your advertisement and how best to get them to see it. A good example is the technology section of a local newspaper, which would provide an excellent avenue for computer stores, Internet service providers and other high-tech businesses who want to reach a very specific audience. Most newspapers will be able to give you a profile of the people that read the different sections of their paper. This information will generally include their age groups, general employment, degree of affluence and their interests. This information can be used as a guide only, and it should not be treated as gospel fact. Remember that it is being used to sell you the advertising space.

The main point I am making is that when advertising in newspapers you have the opportunity to reach the general reading public, or to target specific members of the reading public. Think about your advertisement and who it is you want to see it. This way you will increase the chances of your advertisement producing better results.

7 Size does count

When it comes to deciding how big to make your newspaper advertisement, it is worth remembering that the larger the advertisement the more people will see it and subsequently read it. Of course the down side to this is that the bigger the advertisement the more it will cost.

Recently a client of mine placed an advertisement in a local newspaper. The size was about that of two business cards. It was for a tourist-based attraction, promoting a special discount being offered on a product. The response was reasonably good with about 100 direct sales attributed to the advertisement. The business placed the same advertisement in the newspaper two weeks later, but due to an internal error it ended up being twice the original size. All the other details—the position in the paper, the message, the design etc.—were identical. This time the business received 400 direct sales as a result. In this case the value of the larger advertisement became apparent.

The downside to this is that I have seen numerous businesses take out full-page advertisements and receive virtually no response—an expensive exercise. In these cases I believe it was the subject matter or the layout of the advertisement that did not work rather than the size. There is a degree of credibility in doing larger advertisements. It makes your business look bigger and, to a large degree, secure. Hence, large national companies tend to do full-page advertisements.

My advice is to make your advertisement as large as you can comfortably afford. Don't try and cram heaps of information into a small space. Once you have decided on the size you are comfortable with spend time planning a good advertisement. Unfortunately this is the part that is often overlooked.

I also believe that it is good to experiment with different sized advertisements. Clearly though you will need to be prepared to have varying results. As mentioned throughout this book, advertising is not an exact science, it is often more important to be persistent rather than academic.

Next time you are reading a newspaper flag each advertisement that catches your attention with some note paper. It will make it interesting when you flick back through the pages to take note of both the position and the size of the advertisements that caught your attention. Odds on, they will have caught the attention of other readers as well. Then go back and read every advertisement in the newspaper—from cover to cover. See if you can find some good advertisements that were simply lost because they were too small or in the wrong place within the newspaper.

After doing this a couple of times you will soon get a feeling for the types of advertisements that really stand out and, subsequently, those that don't work. Model your own advertisements accordingly.

8 You pay for more readers

As a general rule the more people that read a newspaper the more it will cost for space. Sunday newspapers tend to have very large readerships (circulation) and, as a result, they are generally the most expensive publications in which to advertise. All weekend newspapers tend to attract a premium because not only do more people read them but the readers also generally have more time to read the newspaper, increasing the chances of advertisements being read.

When it comes to planning your advertising the decision you need to make is about the day on which you want to advertise. Clearly, a big advertisement on the weekend will cost significantly more than a small advertisement placed on a Monday. However, far more readers will see your advertisement with the first option.

I believe it is best to go for a larger advertisement on the higher circulation days. Far too often I have seen businesses waste a lot of money by taking a lot of smaller advertisements at off peak or on low readership days. Then the business owners tend to become disgruntled and blame the newspaper for them not achieving their expectations in terms of the returned results.

All newspapers will supply you with their circulation figures and if they don't you are quite entitled to ask for them. There are different ways, though, that these figures can be supplied. For example, some newspapers will simply give you the number of newspapers printed each day and some will give you the total numbers of papers sold each day. The third option is when newspapers do some market research to see how many people actually read the paper, such as whether a newspaper sold to a family of four adults is read by all four people. This research may then indicate that every paper is read by four people. The total number printed is then multiplied by this figure to give readership figures.

When comparing newspapers be certain to compare apples with apples, remembering that everyone will tell you that their newspaper is the best. At the end of the day, a general rule of thumb is that the more your advertisement costs, the more people who may see it.

9 Newspaper inserts—big results but pick your time

Newspaper insert literally means having your business's promotional brochure put inside the newspaper. Most of us are familiar with opening the paper to find a bundle of brochures and sales catalogues. For some people they are a form of irritation so they get thrown straight into the rubbish bin, for others they are the highlight of the daily newspaper.

There is no doubt that a proportion of readers will never read the material inserted into newspapers and for some businesses, this makes them less effective as advertising tools. The reality is that all advertising has a miss ratio—those people that won't see the advertising or acknowledge it. Newspaper inserts are really no higher or lower on the miss ratio and it is difficult to find statistics to provide a clear cut overview on whether they are more or less effective.

The real advantages of newspaper inserts is that they do stand out from the other information in the newspaper. You can include a lot of information in a catalogue that would be hard to impart in a single advertisement in the same paper. I have used newspaper inserts for restaurants, shopping centres, telecommunications companies, accounting firms and even tourist based businesses. The results have always been excellent even though my clients have been dubious due to the cost of producing the brochures and then inserting them.

The real key to making newspaper inserts work is to catch the reader's attention. A lot of large retail chains use inserts regularly—normally coinciding with peak shopping periods such as Christmas, Mother's Day, End of Year sales and so on. For this reason, loyal shoppers tend to look for the catalogues from their favourite retailers in anticipation of finding items of interest or the ever enticing bargain.

Most newspapers will let you place inserts in their publications. The normal way to pay for this is a price per thousand inserts. As a general rule, costs are between $50 and $100 per thousand brochures inserted. You can normally do inserts for the entire print run of a newspaper or part runs. Of course when doing part runs it is harder to determine where they will end up.

Likewise, most free newspapers delivered directly to households will let you do either full or part inserts, and you can even determine the suburbs you would like to receive your brochures. This is highly beneficial for businesses that rely on attracting customers from the suburbs close by.

A word of warning, though, it is more and more common for inserts to be done mechanically as part of the printing process. There was a time when they were all inserted by hand, which meant the type of insert you used didn't really matter. With the use of machines to do the inserting there are much stricter parameters for the dimensions of inserted material, so it makes good sense to talk to the newspaper before you print up 100 000 catalogues, only to have them rejected as unsuitable for inserting.

The best advice I can give is to design your catalogues or brochures so they will catch the reader's attention. Use big bold headings and bright colours (or go the other way and do them in black and white for effect), make them easy to read and give the customers all of the details they need to motivate them to buy your products.

Planning the timing of your insert is also important. For example, I have seen companies putting inserts into newspapers during the middle of holiday periods and the results have been less than perfect to say the least. The reasons for this could be many—from badly designed catalogues to the fact that half the potential readers have gone away on holiday. The point I am making here is to think about when you are planning to put your insert into the newspaper.

Deciding on the right day of the week is just as important. Weekend papers tend to work well because readers are more relaxed, having more time to sit back and enjoy reading their paper. Check with the newspaper to see if they are planning any features that you may be able to piggyback on. For example, if the newspaper is planning a travel feature on Alaska it would be an opportune time for a travel agent to insert a brochure on trips to Alaska in the same paper.

There are lots of options like this to consider and it is worth putting some solid planning into maximising all aspects of your newspaper insert campaign. When doing an insert it is worth advertising in other areas (such as television and radio) to tell people to look for the insert in the forthcoming newspaper. This will increase the results and get people who are interested in your products or service to keep an eye out for your catalogue or brochure in the coming paper.

10 Establish credibility by using newspaper advertising

'If it's in print it's true.' Well, I don't think any of us necessarily believe this line these days, in fact the opposite is probably more often true. Today's newspaper readers are more sceptical about what they read but old habits do die hard. Because journalism has entered a new age of responsibility, where reporting has to be accurate for fear of legal repercussions, advertisements in newspapers seem to have a certain air of credibility by association.

As consumers we are constantly evaluating the businesses we see on the television, in the newspaper and on the radio. Most of this evaluation is done on a subconscious level and it is at this level that we form our opinions. The big decision we are working towards is whether or not we feel a particular business is credible enough for us to use.

Advertising in newspapers is excellent for forming that credibility. The tabloid still has strong credibility building power, even if readers are not as gullible as we all were a few decades ago. By advertising your business in the newspaper people will begin to form opinions about your business and if your advertisements are good, these opinions will be favourable. For some businesses this benefit is not considered when planning their advertising. They form their opinions on whether or not an advertisement works simply by the immediate results.

I have observed that the more a business advertises over a period of time, the better the results become. I ran a newspaper advertising campaign for a telecommunications business several years ago. We ran the same advertisement every Saturday over an eight-week period. Every week the results got better and better. The same advertisement, the same day, the same position in the newspaper, yet the weekly results kept getting better and better. I believe the repetitive nature of the advertisement not only meant more people saw the advertisement more often, but also the firm's credibility increased each week.

The point I am making is that there are a lot of benefits associated with newspaper advertising. While some may at first be less apparent than others, they are there none the less.

11 Don't underestimate the power of the classifieds

I am a firm believer in the value of advertising in the classified section of the newspaper. By this I don't mean the small advertisements in the 'for sale' section of the classifieds but rather the sections of the classifieds that contain public notices and tender options. For example, people reading public notices are generally interested in what is going on in a particular city. There is a lot of information about new projects and events that can be gleaned from this section of the paper. It is also an excellent area to educate people about your business's products and services.

My company prepares a lot of tenders for other businesses. By advertising our services in the 'tender' section of the classifieds we attract a lot of business from organisations that want help preparing their tender documents to win projects.

A lot of people read the various sections of the classifieds and they provide an inexpensive advertising option for many kinds of businesses. Have a glance through your local newspaper to see if there are advertising opportunities for your business to attract new customers from the classified section.

Notes

Advertising action list

Things to do   **Completed**

1. ....

2. ....

3. ....

4. ....

5. ....

6. ....

7. ....

8. ....

9. ....

10. ....

3 | Making television advertising work for you

Television advertising is the most accessible and the most influential form of advertising. There are not too many consumers who don't spend some time watching television during their day. To say that a lot of businesses advertise on television is an understatement as this media really is the number one in terms of usage. To create a television commercial that is effective is not necessarily a hard thing to do, however, like all advertising there is a right way and a wrong way to go about it.

One comment I would like to make up front is that to be successful at television advertising I truly believe you have to spend some time watching television. You need to get a feel for the types of commercials being aired, how often they are aired, what types of businesses are advertising and which ones have been advertising for a long time. While being told to watch television may sound like heaven for some people for others it is a chore. Put it down to market research and a driving desire to make your business successful.

In this section I look at all aspects of television advertising, from producing a television commercial to buying airtime:

#12   What are you trying to sell?
#13   The steps to making a good television commercial
#14   Keep a notepad by the television
#15   Sell the benefits to the consumer

12 What are you trying to sell?

The first priority of any television advertising is to be clear about what you are trying to sell. All too often television commercials (and many other forms of advertising) send very cluttered and confusing messages to their targeted audience, basically rendering the commercial a complete and utter waste of time and money.

The first part of any television advertising campaign is to establish exactly what you are trying to achieve from the campaign and, of course, what you are trying to sell. The clearer your goals and objectives are the greater the chance your television advertising campaign will be a success.

In recent years there has been a move towards simple commercials promoting one key aspect of a business or one specific product. The reason for this is simply that there are so many advertising messages being bombarded on consumers that one well-sold point has a far greater chance of sinking in than half a dozen points fired at the consumer.

When it comes to deciding what you want to sell there are a number of options. You may want to promote your business generally. If you own a radiator repair shop it is unlikely you will sell specific products but you will want more people to be aware of your service, or you may have a special offer, such as a free cooling test prior to Christmas, that you want to let them know about. Decide which message you want to promote before you make your commercial.

Before commencing any advertising, take some time to write down your objectives so they are clear in your own mind. The importance of this cannot be overstated.

13 The steps to making a good television commercial

To make a television commercial there are certain do's and don'ts. These are the steps I take whenever my company is producing a television commercial:

1. determine exactly what we are trying to sell
2. establish why customers should buy the product
3. determine what kind of commercial it will be—moving pictures, text only, what type of music (if any) and the type of voice for the voiceover
4. write the copy for the commercial
5. put the pictures to the words
6. decide on the talent (or models) to go in the commercial— if any
7. show the plan to the client for comment
8. shoot and edit the commercial with a production company or television station
9. test the commercial on a viewing audience that is typical of the targeted demographics
10. make any changes according to the viewing audience feedback.

For small accounts and budget-restricted commercials television stations offer to produce commercials for a minimal charge. They want to sell the airtime, which is where they make their money so the production is usually a secondary consideration. For larger commercials a production company is usually hired as the budgets are much larger, running into tens or even hundreds of thousands of dollars. Dollar for dollar many big budget commercials are far more expensive to make than feature films. When you consider that a 30-second commercial may cost $300 000 to produce the mind starts to boggle.

Like all advertising, it takes a while to get the hang of this medium. There are plenty of people who can help you put a commercial together but it is important you are clear about your goals and objectives, what you want from the commercial. The clearer you are the better the outcome will be. If you have to make a lot of changes during or after the production it can be expensive so this is why you have to be pedantic about what you want.

When working with television commercial companies be very certain up front of what you will get for your money and when you will get it. I have seen a lot of bitter disputes when the grey areas rear their ugly heads in the production process. Comments like, 'I thought', and 'You said', get bandied about. Have all the terms about what you will get and when you will get it written in black and white before commencing and you should have no problems at all.

14 Keep a notepad by the television

If you are planning on doing television advertising to attract more customers for your business it pays to do your homework. Part of this homework is watching television to see what other businesses are doing. I suggest keeping a notepad and pen handy whenever you are watching television to make notes about commercials that attract your attention.

You may like the style of a particular commercial, the colours, the sound (or the voiceover) or even the time slot when the commercial is aired. Behind every commercial you see there are a lot of people that have generally put a lot of thought into the project with the one main aim of making it successful.

I even go one step further and record a couple of hours of prime time television to watch at my leisure. Of course most people think I am crazy to fast forward the television shows and watch the commercials but the information I collect is invaluable.

I recommend that anyone faced with the responsibility of any advertising should start an ideas box, where you keep samples of all advertisements, letters, brochures and packaging that catches your eye. Use these ideas to develop your own material. Clearly the aim here is to get you thinking about how other successful businesses approach this somewhat complex task. Your television commercial notepad/s should be kept in your ideas box for later reference.

Become a student of advertising and use the information you collect to make your own advertising even better.

15 Sell the benefits to the consumer

Selling the benefits to the consumer is one of those terms that is thrown around with gay abandon but it is rarely followed through. When you are planning a television commercial you need to be able to look at it from a potential customer's point of view. What is in it for them? Why should they use your business?

The following is a list of some of the most common benefits to a customer that can be featured in a television commercial:

1. selling a product that is on special will result in saving the customer money
2. introducing a new service or product that customers may have a need for
3. changes to a business location (we have moved to bigger and better premises)
4. selling credibility—if you use our business you will be 100 per cent happy with the end result
5. selling a seasonal product, such as air conditioners in summer
6. promoting a cost-effective option to other products/services
7. promoting a convenient aspect of a business, such as open long hours, easy parking.

Of course there are a lot of other benefits that can be promoted but these will give you some direction. Anyone viewing a television commercial wants to know what's in it for them. When planning your television commercial make sure you keep asking this question throughout the process.

As mentioned at the beginning of this section, I recommend you spend some time watching television, with a notepad handy, to detail what you see on television. Make note of how many television commercials waste opportunity by spending all of their airtime telling you about themselves not what the benefits are for you.

16 Make your television commercial stand out from the crowd

Most people are very surprised when they stop and think about the tens of thousands of visual and audio messages they encounter—the sheer enormity of the amount of advertising that they see on a daily basis. The reason for making this point is to emphasise the importance of making any advertising stand out from the crowd.

Television is the most visually stimulating of all advertising media. In any hour there may be upwards of 50 commercials aired during the programme scheduled. So each television commercial is competing with the other commercials, the actual programme, the kids wanting to be fed, the telephone ringing, visits to the toilet and so on. Hence it is important to make your television commercial stand out from the vast sea of competing distractions.

One of the best ways you can get attention is to ask a question in the opening stage of the commercial. Human nature makes us want to respond to a question and it automatically makes us pay attention. For this reason a good, strong opening image is very important and this includes the sound, which is equally important. The voice used in your commercial will either command attention or it will be lost in the clutter of other messages.

Most television commercials are 30 seconds long so there is little time to play with. Getting attention is the priority and once you have the viewer's attention you need to keep it. This is done by keeping the viewer interested in what you have to say. Keep it simple, keep it clear and make sure the commercial has impact all the way through.

17 What are demographics and how can you use them?

Demographics is the name given to information about potential customers and the people who watch, read or listen to the medium in which you wish to advertise. Demographics are a way of breaking down potential customers into specific categories. It then enables you to target your advertising to reach a specific audience.

Demographic information covers:

- sex
- age group
- geographical location
- vocation
- general spending patterns
- recreational pursuits
- income bracket
- family status
- lifestyle
- other interests.

There are many other categories that demographics can be broken into but these are the main ones. Demographic information is collected by market research, normally done by a company independent of the media.

Demographics enable you to be very specific about who you want to see your television commercial, listen to your radio commercial or read your advertisement in the paper. For example, if you run a sporting shop and you want to advertise punching bags for men, you can specifically target men of a certain age bracket, in certain vocations and with certain interests (specifically sporting in this case). This takes the hit-and-miss aspect out of your advertising, but it does highlight the importance of you being clear about your targeted customers.

Demographic figures can be supplied by all companies selling advertising and if they can't, I would be hesitant to recommend advertising with them.

18 The importance of frequency — being seen

I have touched on the term frequency in other sections and I will expand on this concept now. Frequency simply means the average number of times viewers are exposed to a commercial. Higher frequency campaigns are generally more effective than lower frequency ones. It is rare for customers to see a television commercial once and leap into action. Statistics vary a lot, and of course it depends on the subject matter, but it is fair to assume that a potential customer will have to see your commercial a number of times before deciding to act upon it.

For many businesses frequency is a hard issue to get on top of because it feels like the advertiser is not getting a lot of value for money. Investing a few thousand dollars in a television advertising campaign is a big step for many smaller businesses, and to think that it will all be over in a week or ten days seems like money going up in smoke. I have done a lot of television campaigns for smaller businesses and without a doubt, the shorter, higher frequency ones work the best.

The more times a commercial is seen in a short period of time the more it will stand out to potential customers. Most campaigns take a while to get a reaction from the public, this means it may take a few days for the phone to start ringing, but short sharp campaigns tend to keep the phone ringing long after the campaign has finished. They also give the perception the business is advertising a lot and subconsciously this must mean they have something worth advertising.

If you are planning a television advertising campaign don't get caught trying to make the campaign last for longer purely because it feels like you are getting better value for money, because in fact you probably aren't.

19 How often should you run television campaigns?

This question is asked about as often as how much should you spend on television advertising? With spending it's easy—spend as much as you can afford. It is a little more complicated when it comes to figuring out how often you should run a campaign.

I have noticed an interesting phenomenon when it comes to most forms of advertising and I call it the 'Old Bomb' principle. When an old bomb breaks down on the side of the road it takes a fair bit of effort and energy to get out and push it. However, once the old bomb is moving the effort required to keep it moving becomes much less (unless of course you start pushing it up a mountain range). Advertising works in much the same way. Once you start advertising it takes a while to start working and you really need to put in a fair bit of effort (money) to get it moving, but once you are rolling along it takes less effort to keep it going. Advertising momentum is the end result and this can keep your business growing for a long time.

Based on this simple analogy, to start getting results from your campaign you need to invest more money into more campaigns early on and then you can normally start to back off a little once customers are used to seeing your commercials. For example, if you open a new restaurant and you want to get a lot of people there as soon as possible you might want to do two advertising campaigns in a month. Both running for a week with as high frequency as you can afford. In following months you can probably back it off to one week per month to maintain the interest and to keep reminding potential customers you are there.

The momentum created by advertising can last a long time. I have come across a number of businesses that used to do a lot of advertising but then they stopped, for whatever reason, and they noticed that at first there was no effect on the business. But eventually it does have an effect, and the long slow, expensive task of building up advertising momentum has to start again.

20 Persistence—working your campaigns

Many people take a very short-term view about advertising. They run one television campaign that produces average results and they stop advertising all together. Advertising is like making a cake. You can follow the same recipe time and time again but the end result can vary significantly. The one certainty is that the more you bake the better you get at it.

Take a long-term view of your television advertising and be open to the fact that it does work but sometimes it will work better than others and it is dependent on a lot of external factors. Give it time to work, commit enough budget to make it work and you will reap the rewards. Try different commercials. Swap the shows you advertise on. Change television stations from time to time. Keep working your advertising to ensure you are giving it the attention it deserves to make it work.

Persistence is a word that applies to just about every aspect of running a small business, however, it is rarely considered when it comes to advertising. Persist and keep trying to be innovative and fresh and be prepared to ask questions and do some simple market research to make sure your advertising is sending the right message.

As a final note on this tip, more television advertising campaigns fail because of lousy commercials and poor buying of airtime than for any other reason. So put your attention into these two areas and throw in a little persistence for good measure and you will be well on the way to running successful television campaigns that attract lots of new customers to your business.

21 Understanding how you pay for television advertising

Advertising on television is like most other forms of advertising—the more people who see your advertising, the more it will cost. Advertising in the middle of the night is pretty inexpensive because few people are watching television but advertising during prime time nightly news is expensive because lots of people are watching. The beauty of television advertising is that the facts and figures available make it easy to buy airtime that targets the right types of customers.

The normal starting point for purchasing television airtime is to work out how much money you want to spend on the campaign. I often get asked this question and my answer depends on where the business is located. In a smaller, regional area you can buy a good amount of effective television advertising for a few thousand dollars. In larger cities where a lot more people will see the commercials the figure can be up to ten times that amount.

Once you have decided on how much you can afford to spend, you need to be clear about the type of people you want to see your commercials (the demographics). If your specific customers are aged between 18 and 25 and are mainly female, the television station can put together a schedule that falls within your budget parameters. This will include the shows most watched by this targeted demographic. This is a pretty simple explanation of the process, however, I often think it is a process that is made more complicated than it has to be.

The larger your budget the more frequency you will get. This simply means the more times your commercial will be aired. Normally the television station will also give you some free spots as a bonus to encourage you to advertise with them. However, if one station is offering you 50 commercial spots and the other is offering 100 spots you shouldn't automatically assume the latter is doing you a better deal. It all depends how many people will be watching your commercial and how many times your targeted audience or demographic will have the opportunity to see it.

Another consideration for budgeting is how long you want your campaign to run? The longer it runs the more it will cost. I am a strong believer in airing more commercials in a short period of time than having long drawn-out campaigns. For example, I recommend clients buy a schedule that airs 50 commercials in one week rather than 50 commercials over a two-week period (assuming the same number of people will watch the campaign during this time). The frequency is higher and the total campaign is much more effective. This is a general rule of thumb and there are exceptions to the rule, depending on what the desired outcome of the campaign is.

I am very wary of a package called 'run of station' placements or something similar. This is where the television station sells you airtime but they decide when your commercials are played. Often you can get a lot of commercial airtime but you can't be sure they reach the right audience. I much prefer picking the shows and the time slots and any television station should be able to give you a breakdown of the type of people who watch each particular show.

To recap, you really need to set a budget first and to do this you need to know exactly how long you want the campaign to run for and exactly what type of people you want to see your commercial. These are also the questions advertising sales representatives from television stations should ask you. If you are new to advertising on television don't feel embarrassed if you don't know the terms and be prepared to make the odd mistake, but being armed with some basic knowledge will often give you a strong competitive edge.

22 Buying television airtime

You are ready to start advertising on television. Your commercial is made or in the process of being made and now is the time to think about buying airtime. The following list are the steps I suggest you undertake.

1. Determine your budget—how much can you afford to spend on television over a set period of time, say three months.
2. Write a brief outline on the demographic, the type of customers, you would like to see your commercial.
3. Decide on the length of time for each campaign—one week every month, perhaps.
4. Contact the television stations and ask to see a sales representative.
5. Give the television station your budget and the demographic market you are trying to reach and ask them to provide you with a schedule (a proposal detailing when the commercials will be aired).
6. When the station has prepared the schedule get them to run through it with you and ask specific details about each show—don't go by what you watch, go by what your targeted demographic watches.
7. Decide which campaign will give you the best exposure and go for it. If you can afford to advertise on more than one station that's good as it enables you to reach a large viewing audience, but this does depend entirely on your budget. It is better to spend more with one station for a higher impacting campaign than to get lost with two smaller campaigns across two stations.
8. Monitor the results. Set up a simple questionnaire that will enable you to record information about how your customers heard about your business. This will enable you to determine the effectiveness of your advertising campaign.

9. Review the results, make amendments if you feel they are necessary, and start planning the next campaign.

Even if you are uncertain about whether or not you want to try advertising it can pay to call a station and get one of their sales representatives to come in and do a presentation for you. This is an excellent way to get a better understanding of exactly what you will get for your money and how the process of television advertising actually works. Don't be pressured into buying but do let the sales representative fully explain the benefits and the process. Make the final decision from an informed position. If you are going to do this exercise for one station it is worth doing it for a couple of stations.

Notes

Advertising action list

Things to do   **Completed**

1.
2.
3.
4.
5.
6.
7.
8.
9.
10.

4 | Have some fun on radio

Today there are a lot of radio stations (and I mean a lot). Even the smallest regional centres normally have access to at least a couple of radio stations. In large capital cities there are hundreds crammed into the frequency bandwidths. No other mainstream advertising media has undergone such dramatic proliferation in recent years as radio.

Advertising on radio can be a lot of fun and each radio station has a very specific (and generally very loyal) listening audience. This section will look at the ways to make radio advertising work for your business as well as highlighting where most businesses go wrong when it comes to this sort of advertising. The tips cover:

#23   How you can use radio to your benefit
#24   Where most radio advertising goes wrong
#25   Keep your message simple
#26   Get people smiling
#27   Make your commercial appropriate to the listening audience
#28   The power of talkback radio—the credibility machine
#29   When do people listen to the radio?
#30   Buying smart radio time
#31   Use the radio to get the phone ringing right now
#32   Increase the success of other advertising by using the radio
#33   It's all in the voice
#34   The outside broadcast

23 How you can use radio to your benefit

Radio is an interesting forum for advertising. People listen to it at different times during the day and for many years it was the number one source of entertainment. We have all seen images of families huddled around the 'wireless' listening to live broadcast shows, and of course there were famous incidents, such as the 1938 Orson Welles vivid reading of *The War of the Worlds*, which sparked a national emergency when everyone in America thought aliens had actually landed.

Radio is also a personal advertising medium. People are often on their own, such as in the car, when they listen to the radio. For this reason the advertising message can be made to feel as if it is targeted directly at the listener. Radio advertising is a good way to build awareness of your business and to give it credibility because of its intimate style, especially if the radio announcer talks about your business.

Radio stations have to be very active when it comes to promoting themselves. Competition is fierce, particularly between FM stations in the larger cities. This provides an excellent opportunity for you to work with the stations to come up with ideas for more unconventional advertising opportunities. I have found most radio stations to be very open to new ideas and concepts.

Radio is an immediate and highly responsive media. Every year I arrange New Years Eve fireworks in my home town. One particular year we were having trouble finding sponsors to pay for the fireworks show. I sent a quick media release out to the radio stations and within a few minutes they found a sponsor to pay for the lot and heavily promoted the event, which was a big success. Now they organise it every year. They find the sponsor, plan the event, advertise and promote it and generally make sure that thousands of people attend.

Most businesses are only limited about what they can do on

DUE DATE

Note barcode for your records:

3 0600 _____

IMPORTANT NOTE:

This is only a reminder.
It does not serve as
verification of due dates.
To verify due dates, use the
Library Home Page
'Display/Renew' option at
http://library.csus.edu

Borrowers are responsible for
any fees accrued in accordance
with the provisions of the
Circulation Policy Statement.

radio by their own imaginations. Think a little left of field and you may just come up with the best radio advertising opportunity anyone could conceive.

24 Where most radio advertising goes wrong

Radio is an excellent medium for advertising but it does have a number of pitfalls for the unwary. All of these are discussed in greater detail throughout this section but it is good to know what you are up against from the start. From my experience most failed radio advertising campaigns can blame their demise on one of the following.

Advertising to the wrong market

This is where the product or service is being promoted on a station that is not right for their target market. This is a much more common problem than it should be.

Airing commercials at off-peak times only

Radio advertising works best at peak listening times, specifically at drive-times. If you only advertise at the off-peak or cheaper times, the advertising will be less effective simply because fewer people will hear it.

Overly complicated commercials

Some advertisers insist on having too much information in a 30-second commercial. The more you pack in the less effective the commercial will be in delivering the message.

The commercial doesn't stand out from the crowd

If the radio commercial doesn't stand out from the surrounding clutter it is a waste of time.

No immediate call to action

The customer isn't told by the commercial what to do next. Take some time to listen to the radio and make a few notes about the commercials that really grab your attention and those that don't. This will help you to identify what makes some commercials work far better than others.

25 Keep your message simple

A big mistake with a lot of radio commercials is trying to cram too much information into a 30-second slot. Having one clear, strong message repeated in your radio commercial will produce far greater results than having half a dozen messages—such as 'do this', 'buy that', 'go there', 'come here' etc.—blaring at the potential customers. Deciding exactly what the one significant message of your commercial is, is the main criteria of any radio commercial. Once you are clear on the message you can then set to work producing the commercial.

Next time you happen to be listening to the radio take note of the commercials that really stand out and send a simple clear message. Then listen for the more complicated ones trying to achieve too much. Notice how the various commercials affect you. Most listeners lose interest in the first few seconds if a commercial is not stimulating, clear and simple. After all, we are listening to the radio for entertainment, not to try and figure out what a commercial means.

Repeating the key message is also very important. If the aim of your radio commercial is to get people to pick up the phone, tell them that and repeat the message two or three times. If you want people to come to your business, tell them they should do so.

Most radio commercials are 30 seconds long so you don't have a lot of time to get your message across. When planning your commercial write it down then read it out aloud while you are timing it. Seeing it written in front of you in black and white can really change your perspective of the commercial. The written format enables you to see clearly how often the message is repeated and it allows you to get a real feel for the commercial before it goes anywhere near a studio for production.

Here is an example of an ineffectual 30-second radio commercial:

> Dirty Harry's Chinese Restaurant has now opened on Spring Road. The menu consists of traditional Chinese food made with flair and enthusiasm from former Hong Kong based chef, Harry Ping. The restaurant seats 200 people and it is open for lunch and dinner every day. Children are welcome and takeaway food can also be purchased. Parking is available at the rear of the building and the telephone number for reservations is 3344-5566 and the number for takeaway is 4455-6677. So next time you and your family are thinking about going out for Chinese come and meet Dirty Harry and the team.

There is too much information pushed into this commercial. Telephone numbers are never remembered by radio listeners unless they are very simple numbers, and there is no repeating the main message. A more impacting radio commercial would go something like this:

> If you are thinking about eating out, think about a magnificent meal at Dirty Harry's Chinese Restaurant. Conveniently located on Spring Road, Harry and his team are experts at making sensational Chinese meals to dazzle your taste buds. When you visit Dirty Harry's Chinese Restaurant you and your family will get to taste a sizzling array of traditional dishes that are famous in Hong Kong. A visit to Dirty Harry's Chinese Restaurant will be unforgettable. So don't delay any longer. The number is in the phone book under restaurants and remember, if you are planning to eat out, Dirty Harry's Chinese Restaurant is the only place to go.

Both of these commercials are about the same length but version two repeats the main message—that is, go to Dirty Harry's Chinese Restaurant. The rest is motivational padding but the message that counts keeps coming back. The listener will pick up the point: think Chinese—think Dirty Harry.

Keep your message simple, repeat it and use the least number of words you can and your radio commercials will be effective.

26 Get people smiling

Radio is a medium that allows people's personality to come through. Television is somewhat serious and newspapers tend to be factual (at least some of the time) rather than emotive. Generally radio announcers laugh, have fun with listeners, give their opinions, run competitions and tell their listeners how they are feeling (sometimes they tell us these things too much). Radio is by far the most fun of all the advertising mediums and consumers react well to humour.

If something puts a smile on your face you tend to be a little more receptive to the message being sold. So make radio commercials fun. Use kooky sound effects, unusual voices and be a bit zany. Don't overdo the comedy to the point where the main message is lost, but making it amusing and even downright funny can go a long way to helping people remember your commercial and then acting on it.

A few other comments I would make when incorporating humour into your commercials are:

1. Test your funny commercial on a few people before going to air, just to make sure you haven't been too clever—and hence no one understands what your commercial is about.
2. Keep away from sexist, religious or political humour. While some people may laugh about a blonde joke a lot of people may be offended.
3. Avoid 'in jokes' that only a limited number of people will understand. They are frustrating and pointless for those not in the club.

If you follow the above advice and have some fun when you make your commercial you increase your chances of making it stand out from all of the other advertisements on air.

Another way to use humour on the radio is with interaction between the listeners and announcer. Recently we were doing a radio advertising campaign to launch a new range of organic dairy products. We organised an on-air competition where listeners had to call in every morning and moo like a cow. The best moo of the day won a $100 hamper of products.

Another competition we ran was a Valentine's Day promotion for a five-star hotel. Listeners had to ring up with their best hotel story (no matter how weird or wacky). The best story of the day won a romantic getaway package. This was lots of fun, with callers talking about getting stuck naked outside their rooms, going into the wrong rooms, opening doors wearing just a ribbon tied in a bow (to a somewhat amused cleaner) and lots more. For these kinds of promotions to work you need good announcers who like to play. These types of announcers are not hard to find and it makes good radio for the listeners, so everyone enjoys themselves.

Recently we developed a marketing strategy for a yoga studio. The people running the centre were motivated and positive and they had created an excellent business as yoga is huge worldwide. We suggested they invite two of the most well-known local radio celebrities to do a class and then spend the next week talking about it. On air it was fabulous—lots of laughs as the announcers recalled their experiences of 'bending like pretzels'. The end result was a major influx of new clients for the studio, consisting of people who wouldn't normally have considered doing yoga as a past time.

Put some thought into radio advertising and try to make it fun.

27 Make your commercial appropriate to the listening audience

Radio stations have very particular listening audiences. I wrote in detail about demographics in the section on television advertising but this area is even more appropriate for radio. It is unlikely a lot of 60-year olds listen to a rap station. It is likewise unlikely that a lot of 16-year olds listen to a station that plays classical music. Of course there are exceptions, but not many.

Because of this it is very important to make sure the radio station you intend to advertise on has a listening audience that suits the products or services you are trying to sell. As long as you know who your targeted audience are, any radio station should be able to give you the figures regarding their demographics. Make sure you ask for this information if it is not offered.

Just as important as choosing the right style of radio station it is important to make your commercial appropriate for your targeted audience. A funky, modern-style hip-hop commercial might be a good way to advertise a new night club to a younger audience, whereas it might be a less effective way to tell older listeners about a new form of arthritis cream. As always put some serious thought into your commercial before you even get close to the studio. Listen to as much radio as you can, particularly the stations you feel will be relevant to your demographic and then start planning your campaign. A little thought early on can dramatically increase the overall results of any radio campaign.

Another point to remember is that people are big radio channel surfers, far more now than ever before. Most people will have their favourite station for the mornings, one for mid morning, one for the afternoons and one for the drive home. This means you need good figures from the stations about when people of different ages listen to their station. You may have to advertise across a number of stations to achieve the best results. Ask your staff and friends about their listening habits. Do they listen to one station only or do they tend to chop and change?

28 The power of talkback radio — the credibility machine

I am particularly fond of talkback radio and live radio reads to promote products. This basically means the announcer talks about the product live on air rather than playing a 30-second recorded commercial format. The most positive aspect of this style of radio advertising is that your product automatically gets a boost in credibility because the listeners tend to believe in the announcer. So if you want to establish your product or service as being credible consider this option.

In my home town there is one talkback show host, who has been doing the morning show for a very long time. He has a very loyal audience of listeners. Most are 35 plus, putting them at the more affluent end of the market. I meet with him prior to a campaign to discuss what my goals and objectives are. He then visits the business, meets the owners and confirms the details. I serve as a screen. If the product is not 100 per cent credible neither of us will touch it.

Assuming it all checks out, he talks about the product live on air. Often I will go on air with him as the representative of the product. This works very well and in some instances we have increased the size of businesses by quite incredible figures. It is made very clear on air that it is an advertisement from a sponsor of the show but the element of credibility is established and that is what is important.

Consider the power of talkback radio for your campaign. It is more expensive than standard pre-recorded commercials, however I think the results far outweigh the extra costs.

29 When do people listen to the radio?

Generally radio has two main peak periods—drive-time in the morning (when people are travelling to work) and drive-time in the afternoon (when people are travelling home from work). These two peak periods are the most expensive time to buy because of the numbers of people listening—remember, the more people you can reach the more you will pay in any advertising medium.

There are exceptions to these peak times. Some talkback shows rate higher than drive-time, depending on the announcer. Late night and early morning (from midnight to dawn) are quiet times and these slots are generally considered the cheapest times to advertise on radio.

Personally I don't like or recommend 'run of station' advertising, where you are given a certain number of air spots played at the discretion of the station. Although some will be played in peak times most will be played when listening audiences are low. I always recommend my clients buy advertising when the most people possible are listening. You pay more but you get more. You may get twice as many spots for your money by choosing lower rated time slots but what is the point if there are far fewer people listening?

The audience you target will also have a bearing on when you buy airtime. You might actually have a business that would be perfect for late-night listeners. With advertising there are always exceptions. Any radio station you plan to advertise with should be able to give you specific figures about who listens to them and when. These figures are normally supplied to the station by independent market researchers to ensure they are accurate (although there is some discrepancy about the figures and every radio station will tell you they are the top rating in some shape or form).

Use the information available to get the best for your advertising dollar. Reach as many people as you can as often as you can and your radio campaign will be well on the way to success.

30 Buying smart radio time

All media costs are negotiable to a degree. Of course, the outlets need to make a profit and I think they tend to be quite fair about what they charge. When it comes to buying radio space there are a number of ways to make sure you get the best value for your advertising dollar.

You can approach a number of stations and give them a brief—explaining who your target market is and what you want to achieve from the campaign. Tell them how much you have to spend and let them come back to you with a proposal. I suggest you let them know you will be asking their competition for proposals as well as this tends to make everyone's pencils a little sharper. Compare the proposals that come back and see which station gives you the best value for money, remembering prime spots are in the drive-times and live reads by announcers are premiums.

Committing to long-term campaigns is one way of increasing your buying power with the radio stations as well. The more you spend the more important you are to them as a customer. Radio is an innovative and spontaneous media and if you have a good sales representative they will come back to you with ideas and campaign proposals designed to get results for your business. If they don't—ask for a different sales representative.

Finally, work with the stations. It is in their best interests the advertising you do with them works—if it does, you will keep coming back to buy more airtime. Sometimes things go wrong, mistakes are made, advertisements don't go to air when they are supposed to. How these problems are resolved is really important. If the radio station is serious about doing business with you they will work with you and I suggest you work with them to develop a long-term relationship.

Be prepared to negotiate hard but fairly and remember the number one priority is to get results from your advertising.

31 Use the radio to get the phone ringing right now

One of the greatest advantages of radio advertising is that it is instantaneous. That means people can do something about it right now. If you are watching television and you see a commercial that interests you, you have to then remember it the next day to call the business back during working hours. Radio can get people to call or drop in right now.

I often recommend to clients looking to give their business a fairly quick boost to advertise on the radio. Making a commercial can be done quickly and inexpensively, especially if you use the announcer to do a live commercial. Run a big promotion to get people to your business right now.

I have used this style of promotion very effectively for restaurants, retail shops, mechanical services, special functions and events. A kind of frenzy can be created by the call for immediate action and never forget, crowds attract crowds.

The key to making this style of advertising campaign work is to make sure the offer you are making is very attractive. You also need to make sure you have enough staff to cope with the demand and lots of other little things, such as enough change for the cash registers.

Many years ago I used to own a scuba diving retail shop. For one weekend I had a particular brand of wetsuits on special at a great price—they were normally $499 and we were selling them for $299 for that weekend only. We ran a radio blitz campaign to promote this, making sure we had heaps of suits in stock. We sold over 120 wetsuits that weekend. Now to put that into perspective, we had sold 30 suits in the entire year prior to the sale. Obviously we were very happy with the results as was the wetsuit manufacturer. This style of promotion produced great results.

32 Increase the success of other advertising by using the radio

Radio is a good medium to draw attention to other advertising you may be doing. For example, if you are planning to insert a catalogue into a newspaper you can advertise this the week prior to the publication day on the radio. This makes certain that people are looking out for the catalogue prior to the paper coming out. Results tend to be better when doing this kind of support advertising on radio. In this particular instance I would also recommend advertising after the insert has gone into the newspaper to remind people to do something about it (a call to action in advertising terms).

Grand openings, sales, special offers and product launches can all benefit from using radio to enhance a television or newspaper advertising campaign. Radio adds an urgency and immediacy that other mediums cannot compete with.

If you are planning an advertising campaign on other mediums consider using radio to enhance the results.

33 It's all in the voice

Without a doubt, the key to all radio advertising is the voice. This is fairly logical when you think about it, but often people don't think about it.

A common problem in smaller regions is that only a handful of people do radio commercial voiceovers, so the commercials start sounding the same. But this can be overcome as there are plenty of people available elsewhere to do voiceovers and they certainly don't need to be in the same town as you in this day and age. You can pick a voice artist over the Internet, send them a script and brief and have the finished product emailed back to you, ready to go on air within a few hours. There are literally tens of thousands of voices to choose from and after a quick Internet search you will be on your way. Many companies can also send you a CD with about 50 voices on it for you to choose from.

Some commercials just seem to lack impact due mainly to a poor choice of voice for the job. Before choosing someone try to imagine how the commercial will sound. Gauge whether it should be read by a woman or a man or both? Should they have an accent, a deep voice, a funny voice or some other redeeming characteristic? Do your homework when choosing a voice for your commercial. If you hear a voice on air that you like make a note of it so the radio station can chase down the person behind the voice.

Picking a unique voice that represents your product is important. Don't leave this decision to someone else.

34 The outside broadcast

An outside broadcast (or OB) is when the radio station comes to you. Outside broadcasts can be used at sales, grand openings, special events or a multitude of places where a good atmosphere helps to attract more customers. Outside broadcasts are expensive as they take a lot of organising, and a fair bit of equipment and technical back-up is required on site. Apart from this outside broadcasts can be very effective and a lot of businesses really swear by them.

Not all radio stations do outside broadcasts but it is always worth asking them. If the station does offer this service, the next question you need to consider is whether you will get a good return for your investment. Typically an outside broadcast will run for a few hours and you might get better value from more mainstream advertising.

Outside broadcasts can be used effectively by a number of businesses in the same area. This enables the costs to be shared by all the businesses, which in turn can all be promoted during the broadcast. Often this is better for the radio station as well, as the announcers will have more to talk about during the show.

Value adding outside broadcasts with entertainment for children, food stalls and excellent special offers tends to make the whole campaign much more successful as it gives customers more reason to visit the site. I also think it is important to advertise the outside broadcast prior to the day it is on so those people who may not be listening to the radio on the day will hopefully still be aware of the event.

Live broadcasts are a very good way to get the telephone ringing and the customers coming through the door of a business. There are some risks, but if well planned and well promoted, they can be successful.

Notes

_____

_____

_____

_____

_____

_____

_____

_____

_____

_____

_____

_____

Advertising action list

Things to do   **Completed**

1. _____   _____

2. _____   _____

3. _____   _____

4. _____   _____

5. _____   _____

6. _____   _____

7. _____   _____

8. _____   _____

9. _____   _____

10. _____   _____

5 | Telephone directories— important for all businesses

Telephone directories are a routine part of daily life. They have been for about as long as telephones, but in recent times we have been inundated with a competing range of directories, often making it hard to decide where to advertise. While most directories have online versions as well as hard copies, the telephone directory in a book format is here to stay for at least the foreseeable future.

This section looks at ways to make your telephone directory advertising work for your business by focusing on the following:

#35   Choosing the right directory
#36   Stand out or throw out
#37   Put some thought into your advertisement—most people don't
#38   Big, bold questions need answers
#39   Don't get caught up with what your competitors are doing
#40   Look at your advertisement from a customer's point of view
#41   Don't forget the White Pages
#42   Use pictures to sell your business
#43   Have a strong, stand out border
#44   Cut out your artwork and place it on the page
#45   Dedicate a number to monitor response

35 Choosing the right directory

There are a lot of different types of telephone directories around, especially in the big cities. Some places still only have one but other areas have a dozen to choose from. Deciding which directory to advertise your business in is a hard choice and it is one that cannot be taken lightly.

Every directory will produce a set of impressive figures designed to tell you that advertising with them is the best option for your business, but I would be wary. You can easily spend thousands of dollars advertising in directories that are ineffectual. The biggest directories are recommended as the smaller directories don't contain the same amount of information. As a result people don't use them as much. Put yourself in your customers' shoes—a position I often come back to. What directory do most people use and why? The argument from smaller directories is that there are fewer businesses advertising so the competition is less, however if less people read them what is the point?

If you really are undecided try a test. For one year advertise in two directories and have a different telephone number dedicated to each directory. At the end of the year compare how many incoming calls were received from each directory and you will know which one has worked the best. It is a little complicated but it will remove all doubt from your mind about which one works best for you. Perhaps they both will bring in good results.

A common problem that arises from choice about which directory to advertise in is that business owners sometimes take smaller advertisements in two directories rather than sticking to a large-sized advertisement in one directory. The smaller advertisements are less effective (in both directories) and their business may suffer as a result.

I always ask telephone directory sales people for testimonials from people who I can call to ask how well the advertising worked for their business. It is helpful when making an advertising decision if you can get a strong recommendation from a business owner who has had a positive response. If they cannot or will not give me testimonials I don't do business with them.

I also believe that today good directory-based businesses will have strong Internet-based extensions to their business. More and more people use online versions of the main directories and this trend is going to keep increasing as high-speed Internet access becomes more and more accessible.

So if the directory can back up your printed advertisement with an online advertisement it will have more appeal as an advertising medium.

36 Stand out or throw out

The singular most important aspect of advertising in a telephone directory is to make your advertisement stand out from all the others. I spend a lot of time talking about the importance of making your advertising stand out from the crowd in every form of advertising, but when talking about telephone directories it is critical.

You can generally choose between doing a full-colour advertisement or a simple black and white advertisement in directories, with a few options in between. You also have to choose the right size to make sure your advertisement is seen and then you will need to have the advertisement designed properly to be effectual in getting its message across.

When considering whether or not to use colour (with the associated extra costs) it can be a really hard decision to make. A well designed black and white advertisement is far better than a poorly designed colour advertisement. The best advice is to contract a graphic designer to make up your advertisement. The designers that work for the telephone directories are churning out a lot of advertisements in short periods of time, which means that often the advertisements end up looking similar. As advertising in telephone directories is expensive, the cost of paying a freelance graphic designer to make up your advertisement is really quite negligible and the results are normally much better.

When it comes to choosing which size to go for, it is best to go for the largest sized advertisement you can afford. If you are going to advertise in a directory make your advertisement impressive. Larger advertisements get more callers. This is a fact which the directory companies will go to great lengths to tell you, and it is true. If this is outside your reach financially at least make sure you have a bold listing in the appropriate sections of the main directory. It is better than no listing at all.

Whatever option you go for, do whatever you can to make your advertisement stand out. I cover a few more ideas on this in the following pages.

37 Put some thought into your advertisement — most people don't

By now you will have noticed that I tend to harp on this point. A lot of businesses spend most of their time and energy deciding whether or not to actually advertise but then put little or no thought into the actual advertisement itself. I find this amazing to say the least, but people get busy, they often have limited knowledge about advertising and they put their faith in the company that sold them the advertising (a brave move in my opinion).

While I am not saying you need to take a year to work on one single advertisement, you should spend time thinking about the following:

1. What do you want to achieve from your advertisement?
2. How will you get the customer to pick up the phone (a call to action)?
3. Have you got a good photograph that can be used in the advertisement?
4. Have you sat down and looked at your competitors' advertisements?
5. Have you included all of the relevant details (phone, fax, address, website etc.)?
6. What section of the directory should your advertisement appear in?

If possible talk to other business associates to find out their opinions on advertising in directories and what they have found to work for them. Show a number of people your advertisement to get some extra input and you will be well on the way to developing a well planned and well implemented advertisement in a directory.

When you consider that many businesses get almost all of their customers from telephone directories, the importance and significance of good advertisements is clear. Take the time needed to plan your advertisement.

38 Big, bold questions need answers

I always recommend big, bold questions to head any directory advertising. Readers see a question and before they can think about it their brain is already trying to process the question. Consider the following:

- Are you looking for the best (plumber, builder, cleaner etc.)?
- What makes us different?
- Why should you use us?
- Did you know . . .?
- Why do you think our competitors are so nervous?
- How can we help you?

Of course there are many other questions you can ask but I am sure you get the picture. Now when I say these headings should be big and bold I mean really big and bold. Be brave and use half the advertisement space with just the question.

Every question needs an answer. All print-style advertisements benefit from big, bold questions as headings and I have made this recommendation to a lot of my clients over the years with excellent results.

Take a moment or two to flick through a telephone directory now, if you have one handy, and look at the advertisements that catch your attention. Try to identify why they catch your eye. Is it because they have a bold heading, a good image, easy to read text, good use of colour or is it simply the placement on the page? I go one step further and actually have a telephone book where I have marked all the advertisements I feel really stand out. I use this to illustrate my point about bold question style headings to my clients.

39 Don't get caught up with what your competitors are doing

A common scenario I encounter is people having an almost desperate desire to make their advertisement bigger and bolder than their competitors. While it is good to stand out, remember that your competitors will be doing their utmost to outdo you. Be aware of what your competitors are doing but don't get obsessed with it. I have seen a lot of people going down this track, tripling their advertising budget to get a bigger advertisement, only to find that their competitor hasn't even gone back into the telephone book.

Sometimes sales representatives can be a little naughty in this matter, indicating perhaps that your competition is upping the size of their advertisement so you should too. Be wary of this approach because it really is unethical and often wrong. I think the sales representatives who do this are few and far between but I have been on the receiving end of this type of sales spiel a number of times over the years.

There is a cutoff date each year when advertising needs to be confirmed and delivered. Often a near panic sets in as this date approaches and this can often cloud judgement. Be careful. Another brief point I would like to make here is to follow up on your artwork and your booking with the directory company. Sometimes these can be missed and imagine what this could do to your business if your advertisement slipped through the cracks? Don't assume that everything is okay. Sure you can take legal action and jump up and down but what will happen to your business in the meantime if your ad does not appear?

40 Look at your advertisement from a customer's point of view

Customers look at advertising from a different point of view. They don't tend to study it and analyse it. They simply look at it and let the brain do the rest. It is as simple as that. If the message is too complicated the brain says 'too hard' and switches onto something else. If the image is hard to comprehend, once again the mind wanders and relieves us of the burden of trying to figure it out. Now I am by no means saying that consumers are stupid, in fact far from it. I am simply saying that for advertising to work, it has to be easy to process—uncomplicated.

For this reason if you are burdened with the job of coming up with bright advertising ideas you really do need to be able to develop the skill of looking at an advertisement from a customer's point of view. For anyone who has done a lot of advertising they will know and empathise with the elusive task of trying to get into the head of your potential customers. If you can do this your advertising will be successful.

Whenever you are looking at an advertisement, in this case one that is going into a telephone directory, imagine yourself as the customer flicking through the pages of the book. What will they be looking for? What are their concerns and what do you sell that will help them meet their immediate needs? Write your advertisement with all of these points in mind. As an example let's look at an advertisement for an emergency plumber—the poor people called out at all hours to fix some of the most disgusting problems imaginable.

If you are sitting at home, watching the news and all of sudden the toilet explodes and starts frothing liquid in a hundred different directions, you need help and you need it quick. Your home is being destroyed and the damage is getting worse by the second. You grab the telephone book and desperately look up plumbers. Now what are the key things in your mind at this precise moment? Do you think you will go for the long established family business, with reasonable rates and a guarantee to complete all work within 24 hours? I don't think so. You look for the plumber who can get there really, really fast and sort out any emergency on the spot. And one that cleans up any mess would be a bonus!

You can now see how the two advertisements can have a different impact. If you want to be generic in your advertising it will be difficult to make a hard hitting advertisement. Hence the reason for deciding exactly what you want to advertise and how this will influence the potential customer.

Another example is a pest exterminator. When people call these companies there has normally been an 'incident' involving something with more than two legs that requires urgent attention. So what are customers looking for? Someone who will come around really, really fast and kill everything that is a perceived threat. Sure there are other considerations but speed is the critical factor in the equation at this stage.

Put yourself in your customers' shoes and design your advertisement accordingly.

41 Don't forget the White Pages

Making your business's contact numbers easy to find is close to the top of the list in terms of importance. If potential customers can't find your telephone number easily they will often look elsewhere. If a customer knows the name of the business they are looking for they will often go straight for the White Pages and look up the name alphabetically. Often businesses will spend thousands of dollars placing their advertisement in the Yellow Pages style directories and ignore the White Pages altogether. I recommend a bold listing with your business details in the White Pages as well.

If your business has one of those names that makes it hard to figure out what letter it should be placed under list it in a few places. For example, my company name is The Marketing Professionals so I have a listing under The Marketing Professionals and Marketing Professionals to cover both options.

Likewise, in the Yellow Pages I have my main advertisement under the listing for marketing companies but I also have a bold listing under advertising, public relations and market research to make sure that if someone is trying to find my business number they will be able to.

42 Use pictures to sell your business

We are all familiar with the phrase 'a picture tells a thousand words'. Well this is especially true in the advertising world. When it comes to advertising in telephone directories I recommend businesses actually put a picture of a person in the advertisement. The eye is drawn to an image like this. Research indicates that pictures of people, babies, animals and products all work well.

The real key to using pictures is making sure you use good pictures, professionally done. Getting a good studio shot can cost extra but the difference between a professional shot and an instant snappy is very noticeable. I also think a shot that makes you look relaxed and friendly is always good and nothing beats a big smile.

If you don't feel comfortable about having your photograph in the advertisement you can always buy an image from a photographic library. These are normally high resolution and ready for use and often they can be emailed directly to you.

Once again, grab a copy of your telephone directory and flick through the pages. Look at the advertisements with a picture of a person in them and see how they sit on the page. Do you think that they stand out more or is the effect negligible?

The ideal Yellow Pages advertisement has a bold heading, normally worded as a question, with minimal text and lots of white space and a good picture of a person. As a slight aside to this recommendation, if you have good pictures to promote yourself and your business you will find you can use them elsewhere. Spend the money and get some professional photography done which can be used in all your promotional material. It is better to have photos handy than having to think about it when you are in a panic trying to get your advertisement together at the last minute.

43 Have a strong, stand out border

If you have read this section from the beginning you will note that I recommend all telephone directory advertisements have the following:

1. a big, bold heading, ideally asking a question
2. plenty of white space to make the advertisement easy to read
3. a high quality image, preferably of a person smiling
4. all of your contact details, easily located.

Now I will add another feature to this list, a strong border that will lift your advertisement off the page.

The reason you need a strong border is so your advertisement is clearly separate from those around it. These types of borders also make the advertisement stand out and appear to lift off the page. A strong border needs to be thick but not too thick and it really should be a solid line. When getting your advertisement designed, try a few different thickness borders to give you a choice. It is amazing how different an advertisement can look simply by changing the thickness of the border.

Grab your copy of the Yellow Pages and flick through some pages to compare advertisements and you will definitely see what I mean. By now you will have just about rubbed the ink off many of the pages in the directory, however your own advertisement will benefit as a result.

So add another point to the list above:

5. a big, bold border around your advertisement.

44 Cut out your artwork and place it on the page

A trick I learned a long time ago was to physically cut out the artwork for my new Yellow Pages advertisement (as supplied by the Yellow Pages or your own graphic designer) and place it on the approximate page that it will be printed in the directory. Obviously you do this before the artwork is approved. It really is a great final test of your advertisement's effectiveness.

When you are supplied with the final artwork it will normally be on a single sheet of paper, with nothing around it. Of course it will stand out. But when you cut it out and place it on a page with lots of other advertisements the impact changes dramatically. It may have more impact or it may have less.

I have changed a lot of advertisements through doing this final check and the end result has always been a vast improvement. This exercise only takes a couple of minutes but it is definitely worth doing. The same principle can be applied to just about any printed advertisement with the same benefits gained.

45 Dedicate a number to monitor response

One way to monitor the effectiveness of your advertising in telephone directories is to have a dedicated telephone number that is used only for this particular medium. This is a good idea for larger businesses that often struggle with asking callers how they heard about their business. Although there are extra costs associated with setting up a new telephone line the expense really is quite minimal, especially when considering the overall cost of placing an advertisement in a telephone directory.

I often hear business owners complaining they don't feel their Yellow Pages advertisement is working. When I ask if they monitor where the business is coming from they rarely have and their lack of confidence in the telephone directory is more a feeling than a fact. All of this can be overcome by setting up a specific telephone number. Most telecommunications companies can even set up the account so you will be able to get a monthly report on how many calls you received and where the calls originated from.

I have recommended clients to try this dedicated monitoring system for a number of campaigns in telephone books as well as for direct mail advertising. Determining the end result of your advertising is very important and it can also highlight other parts of your business that are not working. For example, if your dedicated telephone line is receiving 100 calls per week and you are only making 10 sales from these enquiries there may be an internal problem that needs to be rectified. Perhaps your sales staff need further training. Perhaps the advertisement is sending the wrong message, resulting in customers calling about a service your business cannot supply. A dedicated line can also identify the busy time of the day, week, month and year, which can help you to plan your staffing levels.

Notes

Advertising action list

Things to do   **Completed**

1. _____   _____

2. _____   _____

3. _____   _____

4. _____   _____

5. _____   _____

6. _____   _____

7. _____   _____

8. _____   _____

9. _____   _____

10. _____   _____

6 | High-impact outdoor signage

Outdoor signage has become a very big industry in recent times. Massive billboards line most major roads and there are signs on taxi cabs, trains, the sides of buildings, under bridges, on racing cars and just about anywhere else where there is a big blank space that lots of people can see.

This section looks at some of the main types of outdoor advertising available and offers these tips to help make your outdoor advertising as effective as possible:

#46   There are lots of options when it comes to outdoor signage
#47   Decide what you want to achieve from your outdoor signs
#48   Location determines the message
#49   Bring the sign to life
#50   Make the message simple to understand
#51   Use strong visual images
#52   Change your outdoor signage regularly
#53   Outdoor advertising that moves
#54   Shopping centres—outdoor and indoor
#55   Look for new highly visible sites
#56   Don't forget the front of your business
#57   DIY moving billboards

46 There are lots of options when it comes to outdoor signage

Outdoor advertising, as the name clearly implies, covers just about any advertising done out of doors. It can include:

1. roadside billboards
2. advertising on buses, trains or trucks
3. fixed signs on walls outside of shopping centres and other buildings
4. in bus shelters
5. on train stations
6. on street signs
7. at sporting venues
8. on uniforms
9. on bridges and overpasses
10. the signs outside your business.

To be honest, outdoor advertising tends to be pretty expensive, and that's because a lot of people get to see it. Like for all advertising, you budget what you can afford but in that budget some allowance should be given to outdoor advertising. Even if it is only the signs outside your business, budget to make them as effective as you possibly can.

Outdoor advertising really is a way of taking your message to the people who you want to see it. It is known as mainstream advertising simply because it accesses so many potential customers of all age groups and culture, depending where the signs are. Outdoor advertising can also build the credibility of your business because people think that if you can afford a big outdoor sign on a major highway, your business must be making money and therefore it is successful and safe to deal with. This encourages the customer to visit your business.

There are lots of outdoor signage opportunities and the hard part for you is to decide what signage you should have. As with all advertising, the people that sell it will tell you that their option is the best, which is fair enough as that is their job. If you are a new business, a roadside billboard will tell lots of people in the area that your business has opened up. If you need to direct customers to your business, outdoor signage is a great way to say 'turn left at the next set of traffic lights'. If you have been in business for quite some time and you are finding your customers are starting to slip away, perhaps a roadside billboard will help remind them about your business. These are some of the best applications for outdoor signage and advertising.

One final point I would like to make is that if you are considering outdoor signage, jump in your car and drive around looking at other outdoor advertisements to try and get a feel for the positions that really stand out and content on the signs that grabs your attention the most.

47 Decide what you want to achieve from your outdoor signs

You need to have a very clear vision of what you are trying to achieve from your outdoor signs to make them work effectively for your business. Is the aim to increase awareness of your business or do you want the signs to actually get people to pick up the telephone right at this minute? Whatever you specifically want to achieve from this medium will affect what you need to put on your sign.

Outdoor signs are often used to reinforce branding. Large images of well known products, such as scents and fashion labels, typically spring to mind in this instance. In and around airports you see signs for credit card companies, technology based businesses, hotel chains and of course the airlines themselves. These are all well known brands and their outdoor messages remind the customers they exist and this reinforces the reasons to use them.

To get people to pick the telephone up now is tougher and advertisements for this generally depend upon the geographical location of the signage. For example, when driving into a city the roadside is often full of billboards promoting accommodation, in particular standby specials—assuming that many of the people driving into town will not have accommodation booked. Judging by the number of signs like this it must be a fair assumption.

Deciding what you want to achieve with your outdoor advertising is a good place to start. If you are not certain, then don't advertise. Unless you can be specific, then this type of advertising is hard to monitor and hard to gauge the results. It is likely you will feel it is beneficial for your business, and if you can be specific with your message then this is an excellent advertising medium which produces good results—particularly for those businesses needing to direct traffic flow to them, for example:

> # Turn left 300 metres
> # **FRESH, HOT APPLE PIES**
> ## baked daily on the premises.

48 Location determines the message

The location of the sign will have a big bearing on the mindset of the people who are reading it. Think about your drive to work—you are in work mode, planning for the day ahead. You might not be in the best of moods, then again you might be about to have the best day of your life. If you see a sign on the side of the road promoting instant pasta meals it is probably the furthest thing from your mind. But if you saw a sign promoting the latest laptop computer you may be more interested. Perhaps it would be smarter to have the instant pasta meal billboard on the side that you see on the way home from work.

The message I am trying to give here is to think about where your sign is going to be located and the frame of mind of the people who will be seeing it. Often there is no collaboration between the two. The sign is simply whacked up because 100 000 people will drive by it every day. The subject matter is almost an afterthought.

To really make your outdoor advertising work, take the time to sit at the site where the sign will be going and watch the people going about their business. Are they rushing by or walking slowly? Are they driving past at the speed of light or stuck in bumper to bumper traffic? Once you can get into the mindset of the people who will be reading your sign you can design the message accordingly.

The results from putting this kind of thought into your outdoor signage are very noticeable and your advertising dollar will be much more effective as a result of doing this simple exercise.

49 Bring the sign to life

The Yellow Pages are famous around the world for producing high-impact outdoor billboard advertisements. Their distinctive yellow colour immediately tells the viewer it is a Yellow Pages advertisement. In recent years they have become more clever by making the signs come to life. One in particular received a lot of media coverage. This was a big billboard on a major arterial road. The sign was basically blank with a few words in the corner. On top of the sign was a very realistic model of a blue cattle dog, simply sitting on top of the billboard. The text in the corner promoted animal shelters in the Yellow Pages. This was a very effective advertisement that really caught the eye of a lot of people, especially those who thought the dog was real.

Extending your sign outside the parameters of the frame is a good way to bring the sign to life (although sometimes local councils may not let you do it). Having moving parts and flashing lights on your signs—virtually any type of movement, change or animation—can bring a very typical and forgettable outdoor sign to life.

I remember seeing an excellent sign for a painting company. They had the sign written in big, bold print with a simple message and there was a man (a dummy really) standing on a ladder putting the last touches to the sign. Seeing a man up a ladder caught your eye. Every few weeks the dummy would be moved to another part of the sign, which always looked a little unfinished. Very clever, I thought.

In recent years there have been a lot of technological developments in the field of outdoor advertising. Roadside billboards, signs on buses, at sporting grounds and in other prominent areas are all areas being considered for large flat screen televisions. There are lots of benefits to these pieces of equipment; most significantly the people selling the advertising will be able to make a lot more money by selling several advertisements on giant television screens than they ever will from one advertiser on one fixed sign.

In the meantime, outdoor advertising is a great way to bring attention to your customers, so make it big and bold and, if possible, bring it to life.

50 Make the message simple to understand

A common fate that befalls many advertisements is the desire to put too much information in them. What starts out as a good idea ends up becoming a cluttered mess. Outdoor advertising is one particular form of advertising that is very unforgiving of the overzealous copywriter.

If the message is hard to read or hard to understand it is generally a big waste of money. Think back to the introduction of this book when I discussed the thousands of advertising messages we are all bombarded with on a daily basis. Our brains don't have a lot of time to work out complex and cluttered messages, especially if we are driving past them at speed, usually running late for work.

Keep all outdoor advertising messages as simple as possible. Some experts say your message should contain no more than nine words, some say six—it does vary and I don't necessarily feel there is a simple, ironclad rule, apart from keeping your wording to a minimum. Don't try to be too clever or complicated in the message you are sending.

Recently I saw an outdoor sign on a seat by the side of the road. I had to get out and count the number of words because I simply couldn't believe it. There were 200 words on this sign and you had to be standing no more than a few feet away to be able to read them. Now this may have worked if the seat was in an area with lots of passing pedestrian traffic, but it wasn't. It was in the middle of a big roadside park. Now some of you might say the sign worked because I went over to read it, but believe me, no one apart from a semi-crazed marketing consultant would have bothered to get out of their car to read that sign. It was a complete and utter waste of money. In fact, I rang the company that sold this advertising space and spent an hour talking to a distraught sales rep as he poured his heart out about the sign and how he had tried to talk the customer out of it. Anyway, you get the point.

By now you will note that I am often suggesting you take note of other advertisements, regardless of where you see them. Ask yourself why a particular advertisement or billboard caught your eye. Stop and have a look for a few minutes and see if other people are looking at the billboard when they drive by.

Keep your message, short, sharp and to the point and you can't go wrong.

51 Use strong visual images

I think one of the greatest features of outdoor advertising is its ability to really strike your message home. Everything about outdoor advertising tends to be big—especially if it is on a bill-board or the side of a bus. In Japan the Power Rangers children's characters and Pokemon characters were painted on the sides of 747 jumbo jets. It's hard to imagine a greater visual impact, let alone the value of the fresh media coverage for this ultimate in outdoor advertising opportunities. There has been talk for years about the race to put the biggest outdoor billboard on the moon so that every night, billions of people can see the sign!

I mention earlier the importance of keeping words to a minimum. The way to do this is to make strong images as big as you can. You need to be prepared to use very strong images on all your outdoor signs. These can be pictures of people, exotic locations, animals (which are popular at the moment), sexy images or strange visions. The better the strong visual aspect the better the outdoor sign. After all, a picture can tell a thousand words and a picture can also make you:

- smile
- frown
- laugh
- angry
- happy
- think
- cry
- remember
- forget
- be impulsive.

So when you mix a few simple words with a strong visual image, the results can be exceptional.

52 Change your outdoor signage regularly

One of the great features of outdoor advertising is that lots of people get to see your sign. The downside is that your sign will generally be competing with lots of other signs. Because of this the real key to making your outdoor advertising work (and in reality all advertising work) is to make your sign really stand out from those around it.

A key thing to remember about outdoor advertising is that the people who see your sign will more than likely be travelling in the same areas daily. Perhaps they are on the way to work or on the way home, going to lunch, stopping to pick up some grocery items or any one of a thousand other reasons for travelling often on the same route. As humans we tend to get a little blinkered when travelling the same route all the time. This means we will notice a sign when it changes but after a while it starts to blend in and become less noticeable. For this reason outdoor signs should be changed regularly. This doesn't mean every week, but it does mean at least every few months.

Next time you are travelling to work take a few minutes to look at the signs and advertising you are travelling past. See which signs you pass each day but rarely give a second thought. Notice which ones catch your eye and when they catch your eye—is it when they are new? The same principle applies to the signs at the front of your business. They should be kept fresh and clean and they should be changed regularly. This doesn't mean that you have to try to reinvent the look of the front of your business but you must keep trying to come up with ideas to catch potential customers' attention.

I particularly notice bad signage when driving into country towns. On the outskirts of towns the signs start to appear, promoting local accommodation, the places to eat and drink and tourist attractions in the region. Some signs are so faded and out of date they can hardly be read. A new sign in amongst the faded masses really stands out from the crowd. The faded signs give their businesses a feeling of being worn out and faded themselves. In fact, for many rural towns I feel the whole town looks faded and worn out, hardly an enticing atmosphere for visitors.

So budget for changing your business's outdoor signs regularly. Poor, faded signs reflect badly on your business, sending the wrong message to your existing customers and potential customers. Likewise, all your outdoor advertising signs need to be changed regularly to ensure they don't start to blend in with the surroundings and start to become inefficient.

If you are wondering if you can get another year out of the sign, change it anyway. People have probably stopped seeing it by now. Revamp it and make it look fresh and inspirational and make it stand out.

53 Outdoor advertising that moves

There are so many moving outdoor advertising options available I can't keep track of them all. You will be familiar with bus advertising, but there are many other forms as well. Just about any commercial vehicle that moves can become a sign for somebody else's business. In Japan they even advertise on commercial aeroplanes—serious outdoor advertising that is probably a bit out of the budget range of most small businesses.

Moving advertising has an unusual appeal about it. It is almost a distraction that, while not invasive, is hard to miss. It is big and bold and as sign producers become more creative, visually stunning. Moving advertising of this nature takes the message to the customer. It is an active way to advertise your business rather than the more passive way of waiting for customers to drive or walk by. It is expensive due to its high profile and to get it right really does require a brave graphic designer.

Theoretically any more than six to nine words on a moving sign is a waste of time. Most people will only have a couple of seconds to see the image, read the message and put the two together. It is very hard to keep an advertising message this short and for that reason it is a better source for support advertising than a stand-alone campaign. Often you will see movies or television programmes advertised on buses—the main advertising happens on television or at the cinema, and the buses reinforce the message.

By all means utilise mobile outdoor advertising anyway you can but remember to keep the words to a minimum and the impact of the image to a maximum. You can now rent advertising space on mobile billboards designed specially as advertising tools. These can be driven around the streets or towed to one spot and left on the side of the road. They are an excellent way to promote a message you need to get across instantaneously such as 'Giant Sale On Today'.

Think about how you can utilise mobile outdoor advertising and be aware that to really get the full benefits from this medium, it needs to be part of an overall campaign incorporating other advertising media.

54 Shopping centres — outdoor and indoor

Shopping centres attract huge numbers of people. They are places we visit out of necessity and these days even for recreational purposes. As shopping centres become bigger and bigger, they keep attracting larger crowds of people who visit them more regularly. Staff numbers alone are impressive when you consider the average shopping centre with, say, 200 shops will have over 1000 people coming to and from the centre to work every day. This doesn't even take into consideration the people coming to the centre to sell their products to the retailers or to deliver goods or to conduct other forms of business. Then of course, there are the actual customers—the real potential viewers of signs in and around shopping centres.

Signage inside or outside shopping centres works best for those businesses located within the actual centre itself. For example, if you own a hairdressing salon you will get good results from advertising the business at one of the entrances to the centre.

A lot of retailers resent paying for signage at their own shopping centres, often citing the fact that they pay for marketing as part of their rent. Yes they do, but from my experience the shopping centre will do everything in their power and within their budget to attract customers to the centre, but it is up to the business to attract the customers inside the centres to their individual businesses. It's easy to forget that competition between the businesses within a shopping centre is fierce.

There are normally a number of similar style businesses scattered throughout the centre so to have an advantage the smart retailer will advertise and market their business aggressively. That is why the major retail chains advertise so much. They know the shopping centre will get the people to the centre but they need to take the responsibility of getting the people into their own shops.

Businesses within a shopping centre will get the most benefit out of advertising on signage in and around shopping centres but there are of course exceptions. Shopping centre signage gives you a great opportunity to brand your business. A lot of people will see your signage and become aware of your business. What is important is that you give them a reason to remember your business name or the product you are advertising. To do this, you need to consider the number one principle of good advertising: Make your advertisement stand out from the crowd. This is no mean feat in a shopping centre where the consumer is surrounded by all types of visual stimulation, sounds and smells. One example that comes to mind is about a client of mine, a recruitment company.

This company is very successful and they are constantly looking for people to fill the positions they have on their books. For them advertising in the shopping centre is an ideal medium as there are plenty of people either looking for work or looking for a change of employer. As an added bonus they get a lot of business from shop owners looking for temporary staff. So even though the business isn't physically located in the centre they can still enjoy the benefits of the large traffic flow of people by utilising some smart advertising.

Another point worth remembering is that individual shopping centres attract different customers. This largely depends on the location of the centres and the wealth of the customers living close by. If your business is relevant to the lower socio-economic end of town, then it may well be worth advertising in a shopping centre that attracts this particular market. Likewise, if you want wealthier individuals go to the upmarket shopping centre.

Next time you have a few minutes to spare, pop into your local shopping centre management and ask them about any advertising opportunities they may have available.

55 Look for new highly visible sites

The urban landscape is constantly changing. New buildings come, old ones go, new roads and freeways are built and both pedestrian and vehicle traffic routes change constantly. Because of this there are always new opportunities opening up for outdoor signage.

Renting billboard advertising space in prime locations is expensive. Clearly you are paying for the sheer volume of traffic driving past a particular place. With a little planning you may be able to secure a billboard in a second-tier location, which at the moment is not as busy as a major arterial road but in time will become as busy. By locking yourself in to this sort of position you may be able to reap all the benefits of a prime location without the added costs.

Sometimes new buildings can have a dramatic effect on the way pedestrian traffic flows, especially if the new building is one likely to attract a lot of people. Having a sign outside a run down, old warehouse is probably of little benefit but when a redevelopment is done the site becomes home to a major shopping centre and your sign will be in a prime position.

The other point to consider with outdoor advertising is that there really is a limit to how many signs can be put up in one area. A lot of people consider outdoor advertising to be a form of visual pollution and for this reason councils and other regulatory bodies generally have very tight controls on the position, size and numbers of outdoor signs allowed. Most have a ceiling on the number of signs that can be put up in certain areas. Because of this it is much easier to get approval for a large outdoor billboard away from high traffic flow areas. With some clever forward planning and a long-term view to your advertising needs you can end up with high quality signs in good positions in years to come.

There is a business located in my city which stores cars and boats for people while they are on holiday. This business has adopted the principal of having signs in out-of-the-way areas on all access routes into the city. When they first put the signs up they had no problems with council regulations because the locations of the signs were miles from everywhere. Ten years later, all of the business's signs are in prime locations where there are no more permits being given for billboard signage. The business now booms and these billboards are their only form of advertising.

A very clever concept to be utilised by forward thinkers.

56 Don't forget the front of your business

I wrote earlier about the importance of keeping the appearance of the signs outside your own premises fresh and inviting. Like all outdoor signage and advertising these signs work 24 hours a day to attract new customers to your business. Your existing customers also subconsciously assess your business every time they come in or out of your premises, so the signs reflect you.

All too often business signage is almost treated as an afterthought. No real planning is put into it other than to put the logo on the front of the business and give it a coat of paint. In reality, a lot of thought needs to go into the signage outside any business.

First of all draw up a rough plan of what your business looks like from the front. Walk up and down the road to get a good look from a lot of different perspectives. This gives you a whole picture about which parts of the building are most visible from the street.

Next, you need to decide what message you want to send. If your business has a well known brand name that customers will be looking for make it prominent. Perhaps the service you are offering is more important. For example, if you are an automobile electrician this fact should be prominent on your sign. Some other considerations include:

- Do you need directional signage such as a big arrow pointing to the front door?
- If you have off-street parking is it easy to find or, once again, do you need some directional signage to let customers know where to go to park?
- It is a good idea to have your trading hours placed on the outside of the building in a clear and prominent location.
- Do you need some way of telling customers when your business is open, such as a large neon sign that is lit up when you are open?

- If you sell certain brands of products does your signage tell customers you stock these products?
- Is your outdoor signage equally impacting at night and during the day? Perhaps you need more lights at night to really make the sign stand out.

Take the time to make your signage answer all of the questions your customers may ask. Next time you visit a business and find yourself struggling to find your way around the premises take a moment to see where they have gone wrong. This is a very common problem which is normally just the result of bad planning.

Remember also, the buildings around your business may change and signs that were once very visible can be hidden from view by these changes.

57   DIY moving billboards

Most businesses have company vehicles. These are prime advertising tools that can spread your company message far and wide. The bigger the vehicles you have the more impacting your message can be.

I always suggest to business owners that they have their vehicles sign written to promote their businesses. It is amazing how many people actually do see a vehicle when it is sign written. One report I read suggested a sign written vehicle that spends eight hours on the road in a city with a population of 100 000 people will be seen by approximately 5000 people. Spread that out over a week, month or year and all of a sudden your have a very effective advertising tool.

Of course the better the sign writing and the imagery on the vehicle the more noticeable it will be and the more effective your advertising. Most sign written vehicles tend to stick with a few basic messages—the business name and a phone number. You can do a lot more.

Just having your telephone number is pretty much a waste of time unless it is really easy to remember or a special number like 1 800 PLUMBING. Put a bold statement on your vehicle. Make your business name prominent and sign write the front, sides and back. It is also a good idea to put your website details on the vehicle as this helps people to remember your business name (assuming your web address is the same as your company name) and there is a growing trend for people to check out a business online before they pick up the telephone.

Another point to make is that it is important to have high quality sign writing. You should speak with a few sign writers and ask for pictures or samples of their previous work. Alternatively, if you see a well sign written vehicle give the business a call to find out who did the job.

Vehicle sign writing is exposed to the elements daily so it will fade and start to look tatty after a while. You should budget to replace the sign writing periodically to make sure the vehicle always looks professional and presentable.

If you are going to have sign written vehicles the people who drive them will need to adhere to a few rules and regulations. Reckless driving is a sure way to give your business a bad name, as are littering, road rage and breaking the law. Also dirty or poorly maintained vehicles don't send a very good message about your business.

Notes

Advertising action list

Things to do	Completed
1.	
2.	
3.	
4.	
5.	
6.	
7.	
8.	
9.	
10.	

7 | Direct mail advertising

Direct mail advertising involves sending promotional material directly to a potential customer. It is a very common practice, as you will know seeing that most of us receive direct mail advertising regularly. Being in the industry I tend to take a few moments to read all the direct mail I receive, mainly to look for ideas I might be able to use.

Most direct mail is poorly done. This section will look at where most direct mail advertising goes wrong and what to do to make your direct mail advertising work. It is a powerful tool that can produce some excellent results when well executed. The tips in this section are:

#58   The benefits of direct mail advertising
#59   Understanding why most direct mail advertising goes wrong
#60   The importance of a good database
#61   How to increase the chances of your direct mail working
#62   The first few seconds are crucial
#63   Choose your timing wisely
#64   Test your direct mail before committing
#65   Make it easy for the customer to act on your message immediately
#66   Be prepared to keep trying; if it works, keep using it
#67   Buying databases to get qualified leads

Most of the tips that follow can also be applied to other forms of direct mail, such as mail posted to individuals and flyers handed out on the street.

58 The benefits of direct mail advertising

Direct mail simply means presenting a piece of advertising in the form of a brochure, flyer, card or email etc. directly to a prospective customer. When you check your mail there would not be too many days when you don't have some direct advertising in your letterbox. It is a very common form of advertising and it is one that can produce excellent results.

Direct mail advertising is a huge industry and there are many large companies set up to do nothing else but direct mail for their clients. They have worked out the secrets of what makes some direct marketing work and others fail. Of all the marketing and advertising fields this is the most complex to get right, but then once you do get it right, the results speak for themselves.

Some people find junk mail infuriating yet most larger advertising agencies are going back to this form of advertising. For a while it looked like SPAM (or email direct advertising) might replace traditional direct marketing but SPAM has now become one of the most irritating and frowned upon forms of direct marketing. When you open your email in the morning and out of the 50 messages that await you 48 are junk it tends to get a little frustrating. Of course, with SPAM there is the added problem of computer viruses being spread unsuspectingly.

Direct mail has to be opened and at least glanced at to work. We all get junk mail where as soon as we look at the envelope we know what it is, so we throw it out unopened—this is poor direct mail. Good direct mail will end up in the hands of someone who has to make a conscious decision—that is to throw it out or to act on it or to file it for later use. This is what makes it such an effective medium. A tip to increase your chances of this happening is to use a blank envelope or even handwrite the address if you have the resources.

Direct mail is here to stay. A lot of businesses do it well but the majority do it really poorly. Direct mail can work very well for higher priced items, impulse items, products that are not readily available from the local store and for new and innovative products. The real art is getting the reader to act on it or to keep it for later use.

59 Understanding why most direct mail advertising goes wrong

By knowing why most direct mail advertising goes wrong you may be able to increase the chances of making yours successful. These are some reasons direct mail doesn't work:

- incorrectly addressed letters
- too complicated and difficult to understand
- the purchase involves a complicated process that is too hard and too time consuming for people to act on
- poorly written copy makes the direct mail look amateurish
- the benefits to the customer are not highlighted
- there is no incentive to purchase right now (no call to action)
- poor quality photography makes the product look inferior
- too many bits of paper inside the envelope
- too much text—the reader hasn't got the time to read it
- no attention grabbing heading.

There are a lot of other smaller mistakes but these are the most common.

If you are embarking on direct mail advertising spend a month beforehand collecting all of the direct mail sent to you. Then spend an hour or more going through it at the end of the month. Which pieces really grab your attention and which ones don't? You will start to see common themes carried through in the successful pieces and likewise common themes in the poor ones. A smart, well thought out and prepared direct mail piece will always work.

Direct mail is a numbers game, which really means that the more you send out the greater the response will be. Even a very successful campaign, however, will only have a response rate between 5 and 10 per cent, so if you send out a thousand letters you can expect between 50 and 100 responses (and this is a good result). I often encounter clients who have sent out 1000 letters expecting to get at least 500 direct responses or sales. When they get 50 I tell them they have done well but they are disappointed and often they have lost money. So you need to do your sums well to make sure the sales you generate cover your costs accordingly. I advise people to assume a response rate of 1 per cent and to base their figures on that. If you get a higher response rate you will be pleasantly surprised, but it would have to be a shocker of a direct mail to get less than that.

With direct mail advertising you need to do your homework and be prepared to keep trying. If at first you don't succeed, try again. Be prepared to change your direct mail piece. Test it in small quantities first. Send out 100 letters to see what kind of response you get before you send out 10 000. Fine-tune your promotional material and get it as right as you can and don't let impatience ruin a good campaign.

60 The importance of a good database

There are two ways to address your direct mail. The first is normally sent to the 'Householder' or the 'Manager'. Most people see these letters instantly for what they are and apart from a cursory glance they will most likely end up in the bin unopened. The second type is the personalised letter with the recipient's name, title and address clearly marked on the front of the envelope.

The second type of addressed direct mail is much more successful but it takes a lot more time to manage a detailed database. It is worth the expense, though. A lot of people make the mistake of trying to send out 1000 letters without really caring about the details, just so long as they are sent out. You are much better off sending out 100 well addressed, qualified letters to key prospects than 1000 letters to the 'Manager'.

If you are working on a database it is essential it is maintained and updated. People move, change positions, get married and change their names. Time and resources should be allocated to ensure the names on your database are correct and up to date at all times. I get really fed up when I receive direct mail advertising and my name is misspelt. It tells me the company really doesn't care about me.

Like all advertising, success comes in the planning stage. A well executed campaign that has been planned to the last detail will be more successful than a last minute knee-jerk campaign thrown together because someone feels like it would be a good thing to do at the time. Work on your database, keep it accurate and up to date, and your direct mail will work.

61 How to increase the chances of your direct mail working

Advertising is not an exact science. You can follow all of the rules and end up with a campaign that is a lemon, which can be very disheartening. The real key to advertising is to take a long-term view and to have more advertising that works rather than fails.

With direct mail advertising there are ten important ways that will make it work more effectively.

1. **Use a plain envelope**
   This will mean the receiver can't categorise the letter as a bill, a cheque, an advertisement, an order, a job application or anything else, so they have to open it to see what it is. If the envelope is unusually sized or shaped it tends to stand out from the rest of the mail. I have even received direct sales letters that smell (generally of nice things) to make them stand out. Be creative and a little mysterious.

2. **If possible handwrite the address**
   How many hand-addressed letters do you receive? Probably not many and it is quite refreshing to actually receive one. You increase the chances of the reader opening the letter if it is addressed by hand, preferably in blue pen to make it stand out even more.

3. **Make certain the personal details are correct**
   If the details on the letter are incorrect you really are insulting the person to whom you are sending the letter. Get the information right.

4. **Make a statement to catch the reader's attention quickly**
   You only have a few seconds to get the reader's attention once they open the envelope so if you want your direct mail piece to work you need to make sure you have a statement that will knock their socks off.

5. Give the reader all of the benefits in buying the product

A lot of direct mail has page after page of what the product offers, why it is the best, the technology involved in developing it and so on. Yes, this is important but the consumer wants to know what is in it for them—it's that simple. If they buy this product what are the benefits to them and are these benefits enough to justify the purchase?

6. Use testimonials from happy customers

Testimonials are excellent in direct mail. They are the perfect way to add credibility to your product in a believable and convincing manner.

7. Tell the customer how to buy the product

Explain in very simple, clear terms how the customer can purchase the product or service. Then explain what the customer will receive and when they will receive it. This avoids all confusion.

8. Offer an incentive or bonus to purchase

This usually takes the form of 'buy this product now and you will get a free set of steak knives', or something along these lines. This gives the purchasing process a sense of urgency that encourages the customer to buy now. The better the offer the better the results.

9. Put a deadline on when the customer has to respond

The concept of a deadline for a response is to encourage the receiver to act quickly. This prevents people from putting the letter in the pile of things to do and then never quite getting around to it. The deadline gives a sense of urgency.

10. Accept all types of payment to make it easy for the customer

If it isn't easy to pay for the product people won't buy it. Remove all obstructions to making a purchase.

If you try to include as many of the above as possible the chances of your direct mail advertising working will be dramatically increased.

62 The first few seconds are crucial

Think about when you open your mail. Do you read everything carefully? Probably not. Mail is only one form of communication that we need to process each day—there are also emails and faxes. So the whole routine of checking the mail now takes longer than ever. Because of this, most of us are pretty busy sorting the information sent to us. This means we have become good at assessing and discarding it.

To catch the reader's attention your direct mail advertising piece really needs to jump out at the reader to avoid it being deposited in the bin. So how do you make it stand out, I hear you ask.

Firstly, make sure your direct mail has a very big, bold heading that will catch the reader's attention. Ask a question, make a statement or quote a statistic. Then put something of interest in the letter to also catch the reader's attention. Some companies insert products—tea bags, lollies, money, lottery tickets, photographs, and just about everything in between. Whatever you put into the letter needs to tie in to the message, otherwise it won't be logical.

If your letter doesn't catch the reader's attention in the first few seconds it will be a waste of time. Be innovative, try a few different headings and test them out on family, friends and customers.

63 Choose your timing wisely

There is always a lot of debate about the best time to send out direct mail advertising. I have a number of colleagues who point-blank refuse to send out direct mail advertising on Friday because the recipients will get it on Monday morning—when they probably aren't in the best of moods or that focused on work related issues. Of course, it does depend what you are selling. If you are selling holidays to tropical islands most people would love to dream about a holiday on a Monday morning! Personally, I like to send direct mail out so that it will *arrive* on a Friday. My reasoning for this is that people are generally in better moods at the end of the week.

Try to find out what other mailouts will be going out around the same time that you are planning to send yours. I know that in my city the local council sends out all of the rates notices on the same week. Imagine trying to sell someone something by direct mail when they have just got a bill for their rates?

Of course, the reverse of this is when you are selling a product that can save the recipient money. They may be very interested to read about schemes like this when they receive other bills such as their credit card or telephone. So it does depend on your product.

While you won't always be able to find out what other companies or organisations are doing, a little bit of research into this area can increase the chances of your direct mail advertising campaign being a success.

64 Test your direct mail before committing

Testing direct mail is considered normal practice and it is a smart thing to do. Testing simply means trying out your direct mail on a small number of people before unleashing it on the masses.

The benefits of testing are that you can find out if a direct mail piece is going to work before going to the expense of sending it out. Plus, you may pick up mistakes or confusing issues that have been overlooked.

To test direct mail advertising you make up a small run and send it to a sample of a few hundred people. You might like to try two or three different brochures to see which one gets the greater response. You might try different headings and different bonuses or incentives. At the end of this exercise you will end up with the best mechanism possible, one that will produce the best results.

Most businesses are too impatient to test their direct mail pieces. Once they get the bug all they want to do is send it out, often with dismal results. Be patient and test your mailer until you get it right and then go for it.

65 Make it easy for the customer to act on your message immediately

Recently I received a direct mail piece promoting a product I really liked the look of. I wanted to buy it but as I searched through the form to find out how to buy the product I became aware that this was going to be tough. The business didn't take credit cards, so I had to send a cheque or go to the post office and get a money order—straight away I lost enthusiasm. I also had to photocopy the booking form before sending it to them (for reasons too complicated to explain), which once again made ordering nearly impossible.

They had got me interested in buying the item (it was a special kind of fishing lure for those of you who are interested) and then every time I tried to buy it there was an obstacle. In frustration I rang the company only to receive the answering machine which referred me back to the booking form. Argggggggggggghhh!

Look at your direct mail piece and make absolutely certain every barrier to making a purchase is removed. Accept all credit cards, make the order form detachable, leave enough space on the form for people to write their details, have a contact telephone number that is manned and preferably make it a free call number.

The easier it is to buy the product the greater the chance the customers will buy.

66 Be prepared to keep trying; if it works, keep using it

I have spoken about testing your direct mail advertising piece, removing obstacles to purchase, catching the reader's attention quickly and a myriad of other key factors to increase the success of the campaign. One extra key piece of advice that all successful direct marketers give is that when your direct mail advertising is working don't change it. When it stops working then change it.

Although you may start to get bored with the same piece being sent out time and time again, you need to remember that for your customers it is the first time they will have seen it. If it has a proven track record, stick with it and learn from your past experiences.

I also recommend keeping a file of all of your direct advertising material. Date it and keep a track of the results. After a few years you will end up with a valuable library of information. Some of the ideas you may have had in the early days may have been right but sent at the wrong time. You may want to resurrect a few of your earlier ideas and combine them with what you are doing now or you may simply want a way to remember what you have done in the past (and you would now like to forget). The more direct mail advertising you do the better you will get at it.

Always remember, if it is working don't change it until it stops working.

67 Buying databases to get qualified leads

When planning a direct mail advertising campaign one of the hardest factors is to get a good database of names. Some businesses develop their own databases from existing customers and through events such as competitions. Other businesses prefer to buy a database from companies that specialise in this kind of product.

When purchasing databases you can set very specific criteria for the names on the list. You normally pay by the thousand and while they are not cheap they can end up saving you a lot of time and money. Work with the mail list company and explain your needs and they should be able to put a list together that will fully meet your requirements. Some of the categories that mailing lists are divided into include industry type, position, age group, income and recreational interests, to mention a few.

Remember, you should still test your direct mail advertising piece on a sample of these names to make sure you get it right.

Notes

Advertising action list

Things to do	Completed
1.	
2.	
3.	
4.	
5.	
6.	
7.	
8.	
9.	
10.	

8 | Advertising in magazines

There seem to be thousands of magazines covering every area of interest. It is their specialised subject matter that makes magazine advertising so effective. It is relatively easy to determine what kind of person will read a specific magazine, making it a logical task to match advertisers with magazines. For example, if you own a business that sells gardening products it is reasonable to assume people who read gardening magazines will be interested in your products. Likewise if you sell computers it is likely that people who read computer magazines will be interested in your products.

There are of course a lot of other considerations that need to be kept in mind when it comes to advertising in magazines, but knowing what your targeted audience's interests are at least eliminates the question of whether the people who see your advertisement are potential customers. The tips in this section are:

#68   Magazines allow you to target specific audiences
#69   Most magazines are full colour—use this wisely
#70   Use your magazine advertising to collect a database
#71   Competitions work well in magazines
#72   Commit to longer term advertising and save
#73   Always look for editorial opportunities
#74   Buy magazine advertising space on standby

#75   Don't scrimp on the graphic design of your advertisement

#76   Cut out coupons

#77   Position, position, position

68 Magazines allow you to target specific audiences

As mentioned above, magazines are an excellent means of advertising your business to a target audience. Today, there are magazines for virtually every topic imaginable (and plenty that are not imaginable!). The publishers of the magazines realise people with interests or hobbies in any particular area will buy publications relating to these interests.

Being a new-age kind of man I recently started doing yoga. Much to my surprise I noticed in the local newsagent about a dozen magazines targeted at people interested in yoga. The bigger sports and hobbies such as fishing, computers, photography, home decorating and gardening have hundreds of magazines supporting those industries.

These specific publications make it very easy for businesses to target potential customers who will be interested in their products. For example, if you sell garden ornaments gardening magazines are a good place to start. If you run diving holidays pick up a copy of one of the many scuba diving magazines to see potential advertising avenues. There are endless examples and they make logical advertising choices.

Often businesses have a preconceived idea that advertising in magazines is prohibitively expensive and in some cases it is for all except the largest organisations. The larger the circulation of the magazine the more it will cost to advertise. But for many of the special interest magazines with smaller circulations the cost of advertising is often surprising—these magazines collect a lot of their revenue from over-the-counter sales.

Assuming that particular magazines are too expensive to advertise in could prove a real mistake for your overall advertising plan. Take some time to find out the costs. Contact the magazines you feel are relevant to your business. Potential customers will be more than happy to call long-distance or visit your website if you are selling something that appeals to them—getting the message to these customers is what it is all about.

69 Most magazines are full colour—use this wisely

The majority of magazines are glossy and full colour. The quality is generally high and it is getting better all the time as high-tech printing machines and papers are developed. So, there is nothing worse than seeing a poorly designed advertisement in the middle of a stunning publication.

You need to get a good graphic designer to make up any advertisement that is going into a magazine. Often the magazine will offer this as a service and their designers are generally pretty good. If they can make a beautiful magazine they can certainly make one advertisement. The choice is yours but check out tip #75 before you make your decision.

As with all advertising the real key is to catch the reader's attention. The difference with specialised magazines compared with other media is that you know your readers have a reasonable understanding of the industry and in all probability the products and services you are advertising. This means you can design an advertisement that is directly targeted at specific readers. Therefore you can get away with using some jargon in the heading and text and you can use images that will be particularly appealing to those readers.

Whatever your business, whatever the style of the magazine, put some serious thought into your advertisement and make it top quality. Use bright colours, keep text to a minimum and make your advertisement stand out. Follow these rules and your chances of success through magazine advertising will be greatly improved.

70 Use your magazine advertising to collect a database

Magazines are very effective tools for collecting a database of potential customers to whom you can direct market later on. The way to collect names is relatively simple. You can offer a free newsletter where interested consumers can call to be put on the mailing list or they can sign up online via your website. You can also make a free offer where the customers have to contact you to get the product or service. For example, if you sell bonsai trees you can offer a free booklet on how to look after your bonsai trees. All the customer has to do is call you, fax you or visit your website to register for a copy. You then get their details, which can be used to send information about products that would also be relevant for them.

This is one of the underused aspects of advertising in magazines as well as through other media. It has a lot of potential—always try to use your advertising to attract customers and leads to customers who are right for your particular business. There is no doubt that the more you can target your advertising to specific groups of potential customers the greater the results will be.

71 Competitions work well in magazines

If you flick through the pages of most magazines you will see plenty of competitions featured, which is testament to how well they work. Apart from the benefit of collecting names for a database (see tip #70) you are also encouraging people to take an interest in your product. Competitions can create a degree of hype and interest, and the better the prize the better the response tends to be.

Use competitions to educate people about your products and services. If you are offering a specific prize make sure it is logical, in that it somehow ties in with your company. Another option with competitions is to offer lots of prizes or even value adding for your products and services. This may be where the reader has to buy a product and send in the bar code or label to receive a free gift of some sort. This means that not only is everyone a winner but you can also monitor the results of the competition accurately.

Competitions can be a lot of fun. Don't be afraid to use some humour in planning your competition to increase the overall appeal of the campaign. If you make it easy for people to participate and enter and make the prize or prizes appealing and creative, you can start to advertise competitions in magazines with great results.

72 Commit to longer term advertising and save

Most magazines are keen to get advertisers to commit for more than one edition and signing a 12-month commitment can result in very large savings. Magazines generally publish what is called a rate card to show their different advertising rates, which allows you to compare the cost of a one-off advertisement versus multiple edition advertisements.

A one-off advertisement is considered casual advertising. As an example, let's say that a one-off half-page casual advertisement in *Brussel Sprouts Monthly* costs $500. However, if you commit to doing a half-page advertisement every month for 12 months the cost per advertisement drops to $250. So with longer term advertising the cost per advertisement drops significantly but you may have to commit to an overall larger budget.

I would recommend that before committing to a 12-month campaign in any publication you need to trial it for at least several editions to get your advertisement right and to make sure that it will work for your business. There is, after all, no reason to advertise for 12 months if it doesn't work. So paying extra for a trial period makes good business sense and if you are happy with the results, commit to the longer period and advertise more cost effectively.

Another benefit from committing to longer term advertising campaigns in magazines is that the chances of your business receiving more editorial coverage are increased significantly as a form of reward for your loyalty to the publication.

73 Always look for editorial opportunities

Whenever you advertise in magazines you should always ask questions about gaining some free editorial. Free editorial is always an option and you can use it as a bargaining tool when planning your advertising in magazines. Its availability is normally dependent on the size of the advertisement you book or how much you plan to spend on advertising over a certain period of time with the publication. It is a negotiating tool. Use it in the negotiating stages. Don't sign up for advertising and then ask for some editorial, because at that stage you are already committed.

Receiving editorial coverage in a specialist style magazine is an excellent way to build credibility with the readers. If you appear as a contributor you are regarded as something of an expert. To increase your chances of getting editorial coverage it is always prudent to have an article and some photos ready to supply to the magazine. I suggest paying someone to actually write an article about your business so it is always ready when needed. Individual magazines may rewrite the article or modify to their style but at least they have something to work with.

It is always better to work with the magazines than against them. Try to get to know the editor if you can. Offer to submit the occasional article or be available for comment if particular issues arise for which the magazine needs quotes from industry practitioners.

74 Buy magazine advertising space on standby

One good, economical way to buy advertising in magazines, if you can be a little flexible on when the advertisements run, is to purchase space on standby. All magazines face the prospect of advertisers pulling out from time to time and often this can be at relatively short notice. Because of this they tend to have dead space or standby space available for sale at reduced rates. To take advantage of this you will need to have your advertisement made up and ready to go and there is no guarantee it will get into a specific volume of a magazine.

This can be a very effective way to get some cheap advertising and if you look through magazines you can often see the kinds of businesses that take advantage of this way to purchase advertising space. The most noticeable are the mail order style companies that do a lot of magazine advertising.

Just about all forms of advertising can actually be purchased in this manner although it is not desirable if you are working on a very specific campaign time frame. It is an option to save money and one that can be considered depending on your needs.

75 Don't scrimp on the graphic design of your advertisement

I mentioned the importance of making your advertisement stand out earlier in this and other sections and I would now like to take this one step further. If you are going to spend considerable money on an advertisement in a magazine or anywhere, don't scrimp on the graphic design. Good graphic designers are simply incredible and are worth their weight in gold.

We use a very talented lady called Susan Jones for all of our design work and she constantly amazes me with her creativity and fresh approach. I can be stewing over a concept for days but when I give her a brief, hey presto—perfect.

Having the one graphic designer working on all of your advertising and promotional material has many benefits. They get to know what you like and what you don't like, they have all of your images and logos on file and the longer you work together the greater their understanding and feel for your business.

Graphic design really is the cheapest part of advertising and I am constantly amazed at how many businesses (particularly large ones) scrimp on this area. Why bother? If the advertisement doesn't work you have wasted a lot more money than the cost of getting the artwork done. Typically this is false economy.

Find a graphic designer you like, develop a relationship with them and be open to their suggestions and creative input and your advertising will ultimately be more effective and you will attract more customers. A beautiful story I think.

76 Cut out coupons

Cut out coupons can work well in magazine advertising (and for that matter in newspaper magazines). They tend to be mini advertisements that require some form of follow up. 'Send this coupon in and you will receive . . .', or 'Take this coupon to [such and such a place] and receive a discount'.

Some consumers are very coupon orientated and they literally cut out every coupon they can. Others are a little more laid back about the whole deal, preferring to only cut out coupons of particular interest. Some people never cut out a coupon in their lifetime. By utilising coupons you are able to focus on the market that is likely to action them. This is a good market segment because if they will go to the trouble of cutting out a coupon they are far more likely to follow up on it.

Coupons, like all printed advertisements, need very bold and distinctive headings to get a response. They need a degree of white space to make the information easy to read and they need to be positioned well on the page to make them easy to cut out. For example it is better if a coupon is close to the outside edge of a page rather than next to the spine where people are less likely to cut it out.

The way to make something look like a coupon is simply to put a dotted line border around the outside of the advertisement and perhaps include a picture of a pair of scissors along the dotted line border. This is the accepted way that graphic designers use to create the coupon look and consumers understand this concept very well.

Coupons can also be done as inserts stapled into a magazine with a perforated edge which the customer simply tears off. This is a good option if you want to include more than one coupon in a magazine as it allows for more than one reader to grab a coupon.

77 Position, position, position

When it comes to effective advertising position is everything. This is one of the oldest principles of advertising and every few years it goes in and out of fashion but the reality keeps coming back. I can only talk from my own experiences and observations and I have no doubt at all that the position of any advertisement or commercial is paramount to the overall success of any advertising campaign you are doing.

Advertising in magazines is no different from other media. The better the position the more you will pay, but the more prominent the advertisement the better the results will be. Because of this it can be a bit of a juggling act. You are far better off doing well positioned, large advertisements less frequently in magazines than doing smaller advertisements in poor positions more frequently.

You will pay more for advertising at the front of the magazine, on right-hand pages and on the back cover and inside back cover. When booking your advertising it is a reasonable question to ask on what page your advertisement will appear in the magazine. This will allow you to decide if you like the position or not. It is fine to ask for a specific page when planning your advertising but you may find that another advertiser has booked that page for a contracted period of time, giving them prior preference.

Notes

Advertising action list

Things to do	Completed
1.	
2.	
3.	
4.	
5.	
6.	
7.	
8.	
9.	
10.	

9 | Advertising with other businesses

As competition amongst businesses increases there will be a greater need for smart businesses to work together. Joint advertising and promotion of like-minded entities can be effective in attracting new customers.

One of the biggest hurdles to overcome in these sorts of ventures is a natural suspicion and fear that comes from exposing your business secrets to others. But you will see there are benefits to be had from fair exchanges of information and energy and you will become a believer in joint projects. There are lots of ways to achieve joint advertising and I will discuss the best ideas in this section with the tips below.

#78 Form strategic alliances with other businesses
#79 Share the cost of advertising
#80 Form a precinct
#81 Joint mail outs
#82 Share television commercials
#83 Take over a page in the newspaper
#84 Be completely ethical and honest in your advertising
#85 Swap databases for direct mail
#86 Ask your partners for direct recommendations
#87 Increase your buying power by group purchasing media

78 Form strategic alliances with other businesses

A strategic alliance is really just an agreement between businesses to work together for mutually beneficial outcomes. This can be something as simple as working with your neighbour to share parking or toilet facilities or as extensive as joining with a large number of businesses to benefit from the buying power of a big group. There are a number of other forms of strategic alliances and the difficulty with them is simply getting the ball rolling.

To start you need to contact a few businesses you feel could benefit from forming a strategic alliance and simply get together and have a discussion about the concept. Start small and build up from there. The initial meeting may be about you and one other business owner meeting over coffee to discuss ways to work together to get more business for both businesses.

The power of a group of businesses working together is significant in a number of areas. It increases the buying power of each individual business, it increases the number of customers you can share and it shows a degree of co-operation that consumers find appealing.

You might want to create a name for your group of partners or you may simply want to agree to cross promote each other. By just agreeing to recommend each other's business is a major step in the right direction. Perhaps carrying each other's promotional material is the next step.

Throughout my working life I have seen far more businesses succeed because of their keenness and willingness to work with other like-minded businesses than I have seen failures.

79 Share the cost of advertising

When I owned my dive shop many years ago I remember participating in what was one of the most successful advertising campaigns of the time. Fifteen dive shops banded together to produce a television commercial. One telephone number was given in the advertisement to answer all of the calls and the customer was then directed to the dive school closest to them. Most businesses are naturally suspicious of the opposition but in this case it was swept aside when this group of similar businesses, spread across a large geographical area, worked together to promote our dive classes in a cost-effective manner. This was 20 years ago and at the time it was quite revolutionary. The results were fantastic for all of us and it became an annual event.

Advertising collectively is cost-effective. But the advertising needs to make sense and it needs to be appealing to the consumer, who need to be sold the benefits of this collective form of advertising. One of the main advantages for the customers is the security that tends to come from dealing with a large organisation. A group of businesses working together gives a feeling of synergy that can make the customer feel safe in the knowledge that if there is a problem the group as a whole are more likely to respond, not wanting to be tarnished with the same brush. Whether this is correct or not is uncertain, but there is no doubt the consumers' security is a big issue that needs to be considered in the decision making process.

80 Form a precinct

The best example of a business precinct, where a number of businesses come together under the one roof, sharing resources and making it convenient for customers to come to one central point for all of their needs, is the shopping centre. A shopping centre is marketed and advertised as a whole unit, as a precinct. The same principle can be applied to any group of businesses within close proximity virtually anywhere.

I am a big believer in the power of businesses working together to actively promote themselves. It is an easy concept to sell to existing and potential customers and a group of businesses uniting to promote a specific region is appealing to customers. The necessary components required to promote a specific precinct are:

1. enough businesses in the area to make it a precinct—this may be four or five or it may be a hundred
2. the businesses need to be able to work together to get people to the precinct
3. advertising needs to sell the benefits of the precinct not the individual businesses
4. the benefits of visiting the precinct need to be clear
5. a good name that explains clearly what the precinct is.

Similar types of businesses often end up being located close together making it easy to take the next step of calling it a precinct. Some examples of business clusters that can form precincts include:

- restaurants
- motor vehicle services
- medical services
- grocery stores (butcher, baker, fruit and vegetables and delicatessen)

- clothing stores
- professional services (lawyers, accountants, financial services)
- furniture stores
- health and fitness services
- tourism operators
- electrical goods.

There are many benefits to forming a precinct and if the businesses involved work well together all of them will benefit from advertising and promoting the precinct as a whole.

81 Joint mail outs

I covered direct marketing, specifically direct mail, earlier in this book. Another good way for businesses to work together is to jointly send out their promotional material in the form of direct mail outs. The main advantage is clear—it is cheaper so you can send out more direct mail pieces.

This co-operative campaign may simply require a few businesses to put their brochures into one envelope and send it out to targeted customers. Alternatively, it may be more sophisticated—a specific brochure is produced, featuring the strategic partners, and sent out as a united mail out. This last option is preferable but it all depends on your budget.

Most businesses send out bills on a regular basis so consider popping in a brochure from one of your strategic partners that may sell a product or service which appeals to your customers. Your strategic partner can do the same for you when they send out their next round of bills. Even getting together with your strategic partners to make up a discount coupon book to send out as direct mail is an effective advertising tool. As long as the discounts are appealing the customers will use them.

This is not a new practice and if you keep an eye out you will see it is done a lot by many businesses around the world. Work with your strategic partners to increase the value of your advertising spend and the reach.

82 Share television commercials

This is a relatively new concept in television advertising and one I find particularly appealing. It is where two complementary businesses join together to promote their products. I have seen this work well with a butcher and a restaurant, where the restaurant talks about where they get the best steaks from and then what they do to cook them and make them so special. Both businesses benefited from the advertising and each one re-inforced the other's message. Top quality food prepared magically by a top quality restaurant.

The key to making this kind of shared advertising work is combining products that work well together. If they don't the advertisement is confusing and it becomes a waste of time and money.

Often manufacturers will support advertising when one of their retailers wants to advertise on television. The manufac-turer gets exposure for their product and the retailer sells more product. And they share the costs in what is a classic win–win situation.

It is always worth asking suppliers about joint exposure. Would they be prepared to contribute to the costs of an adver-tising campaign? If they can see direct benefits they will often agree and of course there is nothing lost in asking the question. Suppliers are more likely to respond in the positive to these kinds of requests if you submit a clear campaign plan. Tell them what you are trying to achieve from the advertising and what specific results you feel will be gained; that is, how much stuff will you sell, and most importantly how will you do it.

83 Take over a page in the newspaper

By banding together to advertise your business with a group of other businesses you can open up a lot of opportunities. For example, to take a full-page advertisement in a major weekend paper may cost upwards of $25 000. A big burden for one business. But for ten businesses it becomes much more affordable and the potential for success is more realistic. The real key with this kind of shared advertising is to make sense of it.

As an example let's look at a group of automotive businesses. Imagine if you have a mechanic, detailer, smash repairer, tyre seller, air conditioning service, radiator service, auto electrician and a brake repair specialist all keen to each place small advertisements. These advertisements will be scattered throughout a local newspaper. Their advertising will be far more effective if they combine their advertising dollar and take out a full-page advertisement with a big, bold heading like, 'Would you trust your most prized possession to anyone who isn't featured on this page?' Then the individual businesses could have the same sized advertisements boxed underneath the heading.

Small advertisements are less effective in newspapers. This is a simple fact. By working with other businesses you can really achieve some excellent results with your advertising dollar.

84 Be completely ethical and honest in your advertising

This is a tip that really could go just about anywhere in this book. I have put it in here because this is the area where I have encountered the most problems with ethical and misleading advertising.

If you are going to put your name next to someone else's advertising make sure you do your homework first to make sure the business is as good as they say they are and to make completely certain they don't rip off customers. The absolute vast majority of business owners are very ethical but there are always a few around who are looking to make a quick buck at the expense of the customer. Remember that if a business you are associated with is featured on an evening current affair show, with reporters chasing people down streets and over fences, you may get dragged into the same media circus simply by association.

I experienced this situation (maybe not quite as graphical) with some partners a long time ago. I thought they were great but they ended up being con artists, basically crooks, and I didn't realise until it was too late. In fact one partner was a classic. We owned a busy retail shop on a major highway and while it had been a struggle in the beginning it was starting to come good. It was my turn for a holiday so I jumped on a yacht with some close friends and headed to sea for a couple of weeks. Feeling very relaxed and refreshed I arrived back on dry land and rang my partner to see how business was.

To my surprise the phone was disconnected, which was a little odd—'did I pay the bill before I went on holidays?' Anyway, I started ringing a few friends and they told me what had happened. The day after I left my partner had a huge clearance sale and sold everything—shop fittings, the lot. He was very sneaky about it. He had ordered a pile of stock the day I left so he had plenty to sell and he walked away with a couple of hundred thousand dollars. I was left with the bills.

After this event a lot of people came up to me to say they had never trusted him in the first place. Gee thanks, guys. Anyway, I learned a valuable lesson about assuming that everyone is ethical and honest—they are not. It is up to you to make sure the people you are forming strategic partnerships with are honest and ethical. Ask around, talk to your friends, your customers, other people in the business. Do your homework so your business is protected.

85 Swap databases for direct mail

Most businesses keep databases on their customers these days. Thanks to the modern age of computers it is a relatively easy process and one that should not prove too challenging. If you have developed a database think about offering to swap your database with a strategic partner to build up your list. Of course, it is important that the types of clients you have on your database are relevant to your strategic partners.

This type of co-operation can be very beneficial to all involved and, yes, it does take a certain degree of trust—which you are probably terrified of after reading tip # 84. I know a lot of small- to medium-sized businesses that have grown quite rapidly by building up their database quickly through a name swap with a strategic partner.

There are of course far more privacy laws around these days so it would be worth checking with your lawyer if it is okay for you to make this kind of exchange. I also feel it is important that you get the okay from your customers when you first collect their information. Give them the choice to be sent information that may be of interest to them. If they don't want information sent to them make absolutely certain you respect their wishes.

I also swap supplier information with my strategic partners. If I have a good supplier I am only too happy to pass on information so that someone else benefits from my find. This has grown to the point where some of my suppliers have built good businesses purely on my recommendations to strategic partners.

86 Ask your partners for direct recommendations

This is one of those obvious but seldom done advertising and marketing opportunities. A recommendation from another supplier is often very powerful. But you have to turn to and ask your strategic partners to remember to recommend you and that you will recommend them. It has to be a two-way street where both businesses benefit.

It may seem obvious to ask for these recommendations but it is often overlooked. Some ways to make it easier to do this include:

- ensure your strategic partner has plenty of your business cards and brochures on hand, displayed in a prominent place and promise to do likewise for them
- have your strategic partners on speed dial so the customer can call them from your office, workshop or place of business
- have a sign on the wall stating you have strategic partners and list what products and services they offer
- have a card that offers the customer a discount or special offer of some sort especially made up for strategic partners to hand out.

When it comes to advertising never assume. Always search for ways to make it easy for people to recommend your business. This method is a cheap way to advertise and it can produce surprisingly good results.

Maybe today is the day you will get on the phone and start working on developing those strategic alliances.

87 Increase your buying power by group purchasing media

By now you will see I am a big advocate of a group of businesses working together to promote themselves. The benefits are considerable and I have covered most of them in this section, however there is one more benefit well worth mentioning—the buying power of a group when it comes to purchasing advertising media.

Most businesses tend to buy media on their own. They contact an advertising sales company directly and negotiate with them to buy the advertising. Generally one small business has limited buying capacity, simply due to a lack of volume. If you get a group of businesses together to form a club or an organisation that can negotiate rates as a whole your buying power will be improved significantly.

This is not that hard to do. Set up a meeting with your business partners, associates and other like-minded people, who all currently advertise, and determine how much each business spends on advertising and who they advertise through. Form a co-operative name and go to the advertising companies to negotiate a better rate for the group as whole. It really is that simple.

The incentive for the advertising companies is that if their rates are attractive the group as a whole will be encouraged to do more advertising. It is time efficient as well. Rather than having a sales representative servicing each business one representative can service the group as a whole. All the group needs are the rates.

In coming years we will see more and more of this type of group buying. It saves time for all parties involved and it enables businesses to get the best value possible for their advertising dollar. If your buying group can negotiate rates that are, say, 20 per cent better than the individual businesses currently experience they can afford to do 20 per cent more advertising—ultimately resulting in more customers and more successful and profitable businesses.

Notes

Advertising action list

Things to do   **Completed**

1.
2.
3.
4.
5.
6.
7.
8.
9.
10.

10 | Writing your advertisement—the copy is critical

Throughout this book I have discussed all kinds of advertising and how to make it more effective. I have provided tips, suggestions and recommendations to make your advertisement stand out from those around it and to encourage potential customers to read the information contained in it. But anyone who has done any advertising knows that at some stage you have to sit down and actually write copy that is going to be good enough to get potential customers storming your doors.

This section looks at the aspects regarding writing copy for your advertisements and commercials and you can also refer to a section at the back of this book called 'Smart Advertising Words and Phrases' to help you find the right words and phrases to really write powerful copy. The tips included here are:

#88   How to write copy if you aren't a good writer
#89   Copywriting tools
#90   Using testimonials for credibility
#91   Every advertisement or commercial needs a call to action
#92   If in doubt use a professional or do a course
#93   Testing your copy to make sure it works

88 How to write copy if you aren't a good writer

Sitting down to a blank page that you have to put some words on is a daunting task for many people. Even more daunting is the fact that you are paying money to advertise, so it has to work and you are not really sure how to write exactly what you want to say. How do you go about it?

I do a lot of training for people in this area and the first thing I say is that most people cannot write copy naturally. It is a learned skill so don't feel bad if you can't do it, because you are pretty normal. By following the simple steps outlined below you will be well on the way to writing good copy for any advertisement or commercial.

One point I would like to slip in at this stage is that just as a lot of people talk too much when they are nervous, a lot of people write too much when they are nervous about writing copy. With confidence comes the ability to be happy with white space. Cluttered advertisements are often less effective (but not always), so as you develop your copywriting skills try a few variations of your advertisement. Take an interest in what other people write in their advertisements and listen closely to radio and television commercials to gauge how they are written. At the end of the day, all advertising needs someone to write something.

Step 1: Be very clear about what you are trying to achieve from your copy
Expressing the desired objective of what you want to say is a very good starting point for writing copy. Whether you want to get people to pick up the phone to make a purchase or make an enquiry, or you want to let people know you have moved premises, or you are having a one-day sale, be very clear about your message to achieve your desired end result.

Step 2: Make a list of the important information
This means making a simple list of the information and message you want to get across to the potential customer. Look

at the list—is it too long? Remember, good advertising will send one strong message rather than five weaker messages.

Step 3: Write a big, bold heading

If you have read any other section in this book you will know that I am a big believer in the use of big, bold attention grabbing headlines. I particularly like headings that are questions. This is a view shared by many leading advertising professionals, yet few businesses actually follow this path. You should consider doing so.

Step 4: Write down all other information that needs to be included

This includes a few easy ones, but much of the information you will need to include depends on where the advertisement or commercial is being placed. You will obviously need contact details—an address, telephone number and possibly fax number, email and website. You may need advice for overseas or interstate buyers. Plus, there may be legal requirements you might have to state, such as terms and conditions of sale. List all these so you ensure they are included.

Step 5: Answer the question in the heading

If you ask a question in the heading, answer it in the first sentence of the copy and then lead into the what, when, why and how.

Step 6: The what, when, why and how

This covers the details of your copy—what you want the customer to know in order to entice them. If you are having a giant sale, tell them what is happening, when it is happening, why it is happening and how the customer can get a piece of it. A big question that needs to be answered here is the benefits for the customer. Why should they buy your product?

Step 7: Decide on a writing style

Decide whether you want your advertisement to be written in the first person with phrases such as 'I am Dirty Harry and I own Dirty Harry's Chinese Restaurant'; the second person, 'We have heard about the team at Dirty Harry's Chinese Restaurant', or the third person, 'People visiting Dirty Harry's often compliment the Chef'. You also need to decide if you want the copy to be funny, serious, conversational or educational.

Step 8: Keep sentences short and sharp and words simple

Advertising copy really does need to be kept to a minimum. Sentences need to be kept short and words simple. Use descriptions, but don't try to be too flowery or else people start to get bored and lose interest.

Step 9: Put it all together

By now you should just about have the basis of your advertisement worked out. Now is the time to put it all together, check the spelling, see that it flows and that it makes sense. You may have asked a question in the heading and it has been answered in the following copy. All of the details are filled in, the style is consistent and the spelling correct. Now is the time to move things around or change words that don't seem to work.

Step 10: Close with a call to action

The customer needs to be given a reason to act now. They need to know what to do next and they need to be convinced. This is discussed in greater detail in tip #91.

If you follow the steps above you will be well on the way to having a well written advertisement or commercial for any advertising medium.

89 Copywriting tools

There are a number of tools that copywriters use when creating their work which will be handy for you to know. If you plan to do copywriting I suggest you purchase some of the tools that every copywriter keeps close at hand.

Firstly, every copywriter needs a good dictionary. Spellcheck on the computer is handy but in itself we all know it has flaws. For example, I live in Australia so if I am using an American software programme my spellcheck suggests American versions of words that would be incorrect. Spellcheck helps find the majority of common mistakes but nothing really beats a good dictionary, especially when it comes to using plural forms of words or those tricky ones that do have a variety of spelling alternatives.

The second tool on the list is a thesaurus. This is a wonderful aid that most writers value even more than a dictionary. A thesaurus is a book that gives you alternatives for words. For example, you can look up the word 'exciting' and it will give you a pile of other words that mean the same thing or have a similar meaning. As a result you can make your copy more interesting by not repeating the same words over and over again.

Thirdly, a scrapbook, bin or box where you can store cut-out copies of advertisements that have caught your attention is helpful. You can then scan these bits of copy when you are looking for ideas and inspiration.

Finally, I would suggest a book that contains a large number of headings, words and slogans to help you write your copy. One that I am particularly fond of is *Words That Sell* by Richard Bayan (Contemporary Books). There are a number of these styles of books available and the section at the back of this book called 'Smart Advertising Words and Phrases' is an abbreviated form of this kind of copywriting tool.

90 Using testimonials for credibility

Testimonials are very powerful when used well in advertising. Basically they are endorsements of your business from satisfied customers. Large companies use them all the time, most noticeable with celebrity quotes. Small businesses can use testimonials just as effectively.

Collecting testimonials is easy. Every business has a number of customers who are loyal and they are normally more than happy to offer a comment about your business. Asking for a written testimonial is fine but if they haven't got the time to write something down get them to do a verbal testimonial and copy it down.

When collecting testimonials make absolutely certain the customer is happy for you to use their words and name in advertising material. It is a little rude to assume this is okay and some people may take offence if they are not asked. I like to actually get them to sign a release stating simply that the testimonial given is okay to be used in advertising material.

The types of comments you are after are the ones that say how satisfied the customer is with your business, products or services. Testimonials are recommendations so they are even more powerful if the customer states how long they have been using the business, why they use it and the fact that they intend to keep using it. These all help to reinforce the message that this business, product or service is good.

Testimonials help potential customers to make up their mind about using a new business because they are going by the recommendation of a third person. All businesses will tell you how great they are but to have an independent customer sharing their experience is far more convincing.

Collecting testimonials can be time consuming and unfortunately most of us wait until we need them before collecting them—often it gets forgotten or put in the too hard basket. This will make the whole process a bit of a rush when you do need them. I recommend you start collecting testimonials on a regular basis and keep them in a folder. That way, as soon as you do need them they are at your finger tips, ready to be used for all of your advertising.

91 Every advertisement or commercial needs a call to action

A lot of advertising works really well until the end. The advertising stands out from the crowd, the information is passed to the potential customer, they are motivated and interested and then nothing. The advertisement or commercial simply ends and the next one vies for the customer's attention. So, just as important as getting attention is a call to action.

What does this mean? You simply tell the potential customer what to do next. It may be to pick up the phone, come down to the business, log onto the Internet, stop hesitating and buy today, tell your friends, cut this coupon out or join today. There are thousands of possible calls to action.

The call to action is the clincher. Most advertising seems to end in a mumble when it really needs to be powerful and it needs to be convincing. Use strong words that will inspire the reader or listener to say, 'Yes, I will do something about this right now'.

One of the best calls to action I've seen being used is on home shopping style commercials, where the viewer is constantly encouraged to call right now and you will save money and get a free gift. Another is done for takeaway food shops, such as pizza places, who advertise around dinner time—with big visual commercials showing steaming hot food straight out of the oven—with 'Call now and you can have this pizza in front of you within 30 minutes'.

Take some time to make your call to action impressive and inspirational. Spend as much time working on this as you would on the parts of your advertising designed to catch attention and you will reap the benefits.

92 If in doubt use a professional or do a course

If you are really struggling when it comes to writing copy there are people who can help. Just about every town has a writer or two lurking in the shadows who will be only to willing to help write some copy. Just remember, though, because someone is a writer it doesn't mean they can write good advertising copy, just like a good advertising copywriter isn't necessarily going to be able to write a best selling novel.

If you plan to use a professional copywriter ask for samples of their work or for references from past customers (or both). Some business owners use copywriters to check over their work before submitting it for publication, and this is a good option.

Local universities are often a good source of potential copy-writers and there are always a few students around keen to make some extra money and to gain some experience in the commercial world—especially people studying journalism. Another alternative is to build your own writing skills by doing a communication course or copywriting course at an educational institution. There are lots of these courses available and they can even be done online or by correspondence.

As I mentioned earlier, copywriting doesn't come naturally for most people so if you are keen to improve your own skills you have three options:

1. keep practising
2. work with a professional
3. do a course to help you develop your own skills.

93 Testing your copy to make sure it works

The last significant part of writing copy is to test it and to proof it. In my office I write a lot of copy. None of it leaves the office without it being read and proofed for mistakes by at least one other person, preferably two.

When you are writing copy it is easy to get too close to it, to overlook an obvious spelling mistake that the spellchecker on the computer has ignored and to not look at the copy as a whole. Always give your copy to other people to review and comment on. When it comes to making content changes it is up to you whether or not you want to make the changes suggested but generally you are looking for specific feedback including:

- does the copy stand out
- is it easy to understand
- is the main message clear
- is it inspirational
- does it make you want to act on it
- is the grammar and spelling okay?

A common advertising practise is to actually test advertisements on a group of people in the targeted demographic to get their feedback and comments. The larger the campaign the more important this is. It costs a little to test potential advertisements and commercials but it costs a lot if you go straight to air and they don't work.

As a minimum show other people your copy before it goes to production and where possible test the message on potential customers.

Notes

Advertising action list

Things to do   **Completed**

1.
2.
3.
4.
5.
6.
7.
8.
9.
10.

11 | Using the Internet to advertise your business

Now the dust stirred up by the thought of making instant millions from a website has settled, we can all get back to using the Internet for its true value. This section looks at how to make the most of advertising on the Internet and also how to advertise the Internet-based aspect of your business. The information comes largely from my own experience in online marketing and advertising a range of Internet-based businesses.

For a long time (at least a long time in the Internet era) banner advertisements were the talk of the town. To a large degree the value of banner advertisements has been questioned and hotly debated. This is true with almost every aspect of advertising on the Internet. But there are other important areas to look at to get the most from the Internet, including these tips:

#94   The importance of advertising your website in other areas
#95   Give people a reason to come back to your site
#96   The importance of your domain name or web address
#97   Directional advertising and the Internet
#98   Linking is advertising—work with others
#99   Banner advertising—does it work?
#100 Search engine advertising—what does it mean?
#101 Constantly review your website and your Internet strategy

94 The importance of advertising your website in other areas

While many businesses have embraced the Internet and its potential, many others still look at it with a degree of scepticism. I often hear statements like, 'We built a website but it was a waste of time because no-one visited the site'. From my experience the three main reasons for the perceived failings of the Internet are:

1. unrealistic expectations about what the Internet can do for a business
2. poorly designed websites (many look amateurish)
3. no attention focused on driving traffic (visitors) to the site.

Having unrealistic expectations about what the Internet can do for a business is largely a result of the much publicised hype of overnight 'dot.com' millionaires. Many businesses expected they could get a website and then sit back and rake in the money. Of course it wasn't that easy as the subsequent demise of the dot.com boom proved. The *real* value of the Internet is still being realised. It is the singular most powerful tool for dispersing information about a business, 24 hours per day. It is a tool for profiling a business and educating both existing and potential customers. Use it with these features in mind and most businesses can benefit dramatically from the Internet.

Poorly designed websites are a hangover of the medium's evolution. As more sophisticated web design software packages have become available and more people have learnt how to use them, the overall design has become better—speed and functionality of a website is much more desirable than bells and whistles. Most businesses that have dabbled in the Internet realise that a website is an ongoing work in progress. It is never finished, and it needs to be constantly updated and improved.

The final point above, that of attracting visitors to a site, is significant. Having a website but having no-one visiting it is a waste of time. There are lots of ways to attract people to your website, such as via search engines, but one of the real keys to advertising your website is in mainstream areas such as in your promotional material, in all of your advertisements, in your television commercials, outside your business, on your stationery, on your packaging and even on your products. The more places you advertise your website address the more people will be encouraged to visit it. More and more people research a potential business on the Internet before making contact. For this reason it is important that the web address is easy to find. Hence the need for mainstream advertising of your web address.

An interesting phenomenon worth noting, and one that shows what the future may have in store for us, is that research shows the youth of today struggle to use a telephone book. It is big and bulky, not necessarily logical in the layout and there isn't always one around when it's needed. This market needs to see the web address in mainstream advertising to recall it when they are looking for your company. Does this mean that in 50 years we won't have telephone books? Who knows? My instincts say we won't but in the shorter term they are important and you should have your website listed in telephone directories as well.

To drive traffic to your site make certain you include your web address (or domain name) in all of your mainstream advertising, just as you include your telephone number. Not only will your traffic flow increase so will the results you achieve from your website.

As a slightly separate but related tip, most businesses have very little idea as to how many people actually visit their website. The company that hosts your website will be able to give you this information and, in fact, many do automatically. If you don't know how much traffic you are getting find out. This information will let you know if your advertising is working.

95 Give people a reason to come back to your site

If a website doesn't change its information and/or graphics people may look at it a few times but then basically have no reason to come back to the site. Research shows that the best websites are constantly changing and they contain information the customers will want to refer to on a regular basis. An example of this is websites that show stock prices or news. They are constantly changing and being updated every few minutes. Whenever the consumer visits the site there is always something new to see and as a result they keep coming back.

Even sites that don't necessarily have lots of new information can be set up so the front page (or home page) changes every time a visitor hits the site. This can give a constantly changing feeling to the site and in turn adds a higher degree of interest for the visitor.

The other thing to do is to put information on the site that people will want to read on a regular basis. This may be news flashes, weather, a webcam, product releases, a daily column about your business or just about anything else. Make it interesting and appealing and change it frequently and your customers will have a reason to come back to your site.

96 The importance of your domain name or web address

Having a memorable or logical domain name or website address is essential when it comes to increasing traffic flow to your site. If your business is called Bob's Bakery, ideally your website domain name should be www.bobsbakery.com. This is logical and it makes it easy for customers to find it on the Internet. They can pretty well guess the site name or try just a few variations before finding it.

What is all too common though are businesses that have complicated names, long names, difficult to spell names or common names. These make it harder for people to find the site on the Internet and harder to remember the site name from advertising.

The moral to this story is to try and have your domain name matching your business name as closely as possible. If you can't because someone else has registered the name you will have to choose a name that is either closely related, perhaps with the suffix—.net, .org or .something else—so all the consumer has to remember is the last bit, or alternatively pick a name that describes the business. For example, I had a business once called Let's Go North Queensland. This website name is too long so we simply registered the site www.letsgo.com.au, which was available, easy for the customer to remember and easy to promote.

The importance of a good name cannot be underestimated when it comes to using the Internet.

97 Directional advertising and the Internet

We have done a lot of advertising for property developers in recent years and their standard approach has always been to take big, bold full-colour advertisements in the newspapers. This is very expensive and often the advertisements are competing with literally hundreds of other developers' advertisements. As a result we have encouraged our clients to use directional advertising.

Directional advertising is where the mainstream radio, newspaper and television advertising drives traffic to a website. We often do it as a 'teaser' campaign—small advertisements in other media tease people or even dare them to visit the site. Once the customer logs on it is up to the website to sell to them, which of course it should do magnificently.

This type of advertising is not only cost effective as the advertisements needed are much smaller, it enables a much wider reach of advertising. We put advertisements that direct traffic to the website in papers all around the world looking for investors and the results speak for themselves—dramatic sales while highly cost effective. Another benefit of directional advertising is that it takes the consumer away from other competitors that are advertising in the same paper.

We have used this directional advertising in another manner to save clients money. One client wanted to recruit a pile of new staff. They didn't want to use a recruitment company so we suggested they form their own employment site and use small directional advertisements in the 'positions vacant' section of the paper in order to drive potential employees to their site. It worked a treat and saved them tens of thousands of dollars in advertising costs. Whether the recruitment process was better or not is questionable but their desired result was achieved.

Using directional advertising to attract visitors to a website is becoming increasingly popular and it will continue to grow.

The real key to its success is to make certain your website is of a high enough standard to complete the sale once you have the customer there.

98 Linking is advertising—work with others

Links are really the essence of the Internet, allowing information to flow—one website leads to another. Linking your website to other websites is important for a number of reasons. Search engines in particular look for sites with lots of links as it shows that there is significant interest in the site to attract more visitors.

Linking is a simple process that is inexpensive and logical, particularly if you link to businesses or associations that make sense for the customer. For example, one of our clients makes protective clothing to wear in the ocean. Their website links to the Bureau of Meteorology for up-to-the-minute weather forecasts as well as to the Skin Cancer Foundation, which gives the consumer all of the reasons to cover up and to keep out of the sun. This is a logical relationship that works well. Likewise the links work backwards. Someone connecting to the Skin Cancer Foundation's website can find a link to our client's site, where they can buy clothing to protect them from the sun.

There are countless logical associations like the above and it is a simple matter of putting some thought into it. You will need to always thoroughly explore any websites you plan to link to, of course. Websites have to be as professional as the site they are linked to and the information on the site cannot conflict with recommendations or products on the main site. I often see high quality websites linked to amateurish sites and I really believe it lets the main host down. Link your site as much as you can but be selective about who you link to.

Take a few moments right now to make up a list of businesses you could link with your site.

99 Banner advertising—does it work?

Banner advertisements were treated with a large degree of enthusiasm, closely followed by a large degree of scepticism. Now they are treated with a larger degree of neutrality. Do they work? I believe they do, but like all advertising the success of them lies in the advertisement itself.

If a banner advertisement is to work it needs to be selling something of interest to a particular consumer. For example, a banner advertisement waxing lyrically about the benefits of mountain climbing equipment will probably not produce great results on a site promoting stamp collecting (I know this example is extreme but I'm sure you get the picture). For banner advertising to work it has to tie in with the targeted audience. Make it relevant and appealing to the people who will see it.

One way I have found banner advertising particularly advantageous is to use it on my own website. You can have banner advertisements for your own products or services scattered throughout your site. This will lead people visiting your site to explore other areas of the site which they may not normally visit. If they are logging onto your website in the first place odds on they are interested in your products or services to some degree. It will be a relatively easy process to then lead them to other areas in your site to increase the overall effectiveness of your website.

Banner advertisements need to be bright and bold, contain minimal wording and be straight to the point. I liken them to advertising on buses or on billboards. If the reader can't take the message in within seconds they are a waste of time. Animated or moving banner advertisements are good for catching attention, but they have to load fast—too many are simply too slow and the customer may have moved on before it is ready for viewing.

As with all advertising take a look at other advertisements in this medium next time you are surfing the net to see which ones catch your attention. Take note of what aspect of the banner reaches you. Is it at the top of the page or the bottom? What colours do they use? What wording do they use?

One of my pet hates is when you do click on a banner advertisement and the link no longer works. Banners need to be checked quite regularly and expired links are like disconnected phones—a waste of time.

Use banner advertisements to either direct traffic to your site or to direct traffic within your site. Follow the above guidelines and be prepared to try a number of options to find the one that works for you.

100 Search engine advertising — what does it mean?

What are search engines? I like to think of them as the librarians of the Internet. If your business is well positioned with search engines it means you are more likely to be found when people are surfing the Internet. Using search engines is essential to getting traffic flow to your website.

Companies that host websites can give you statistics about where your traffic flow comes from and how many people come from each particular search engine. These facts and figures show the importance of the search engines in generating traffic flow.

There was a time when submitting your domain name and website to the search engines was free. This is becoming a rarity and the norm will soon be that you will have to pay to submit. Just about every search engine will charge you to list your site. This will have a couple of spin-off effects.

Obviously it will be an added expense for businesses wanting an Internet presence but it will generally reduce the overall number of websites that come up whenever you do a search, meaning less competition. The smaller websites will opt out of paying for search engine initialisation, leaving a less cluttered database for consumers. Whether this is better or not depends what you are using the Internet for. If you use it for research you will probably be worse off; if you use it to sell products you will probably be better off.

There are different levels of advertising rates on search engines. The simple way to understand this is that the more you pay, the more people will be directed to your site. Also, the more you pay the higher up the search list your business name will appear when people plug in a keyword.

The Internet is a numbers game. If you sell one product for every thousand visitors to your site the aim is to increase the number of visitors so you sell more products. This may appear oversimplified but the Internet has become overcomplicated and it doesn't need to be.

101 Constantly review your website and your Internet strategy

The Internet is one of the newest advertising opportunities available to modern businesses. When radio first hit the airwaves there were many different attempts at figuring out how to use it to generate advertising revenue. Many of these worked and many didn't. The same went for television, newspapers, magazines and billboards. They didn't just start up and become these incredible advertising opportunities. They evolved into what they are today and the Internet is no different.

How we use the Internet now will be a far cry from how we will use it in ten years time. Think back to the first black and white television programmes where the commercials were all read by the person hosting the show. Change is the one certainty in the advertising arena and as time goes on the products become slicker and more effective.

To really make the Internet work for your business you need to be constantly reviewing your attitude towards it. You need to review your site constantly and look for ways to make it faster, more user friendly, more interesting and ultimately more effective. For those businesses that embrace the constantly evolving nature of the Internet change is not so much of an issue.

The preconceived ideas we have developed about the Net and what it can do for our businesses is the single biggest limitation facing those wanting to do more business over the Net or wanting to promote their business more over the Net. Overcome those preconceptions and accept that today's business owners are pioneers in the Internet field. What we do today will form the trends and standards for tomorrow's Internet users.

Don't get stuck in the rut of doing what everyone else is doing and be prepared to think outside of the square. After all, this is what helped to develop the Internet in the first place.

Notes

Advertising action list

Things to do   **Completed**

1. _____   _____

2. _____   _____

3. _____   _____

4. _____   _____

5. _____   _____

6. _____   _____

7. _____   _____

8. _____   _____

9. _____   _____

10. _____   _____

Bonus Section—
20 more advertising tips

This section looks at a range of different advertising options that don't necessarily fit into the other categories of this book. Coincidentally, they are some of my favourite forms of advertising. Like all advertising and marketing the real key to success is to make your business stand out from your competitors. The tips in this section are:

#102 Set up a shopping centre display

#103 Make some smart promotional giveaways

#104 Message on hold—the captive audience

#105 Sell yourself at the movies

#106 We all get dockets and most of us keep them

#107 The good old business card

#108 Letterbox drop to success

#109 Take your message to the sky

#110 Flashing lights draw attention

#111 Painted cows—advertising in the paddock

#112 Send out media releases for free, instant advertising

#113 Are your advertising sales representatives asking the right questions?

#114 What does an advertising agency do and cost?

#115 Use your business foyer to advertise your business

#116 Remember every city is different

#117 The advertising brainstorm—a powerful weapon

#118 Advertise your brand

#119 Every letter, invoice, envelope, email and fax has advertising potential

#120 Research often—attack magazines and newspapers with scissors

#121 Conduct your own market research to avoid wasting money

102 Set up a shopping centre display

In the section on outdoor signage I discussed advertising in shopping centres. There are a number of reasons why this form of signage is successful but it is mainly due to the large number of people who visit shopping centres each day. An extension of this idea is to go into shopping centres and set up a display. Most shopping centres will allow this kind of advertising promotion. You will have to pay a daily rate and there are likely to be a number of conditions you will need to adhere to.

I have recommended this for a lot of my clients from dance schools to car detailers and they have all had excellent results. It is a great way to generate new customers in a relatively short amount of time, and is very high profile. To make the promotion even more successful have a special offer that interested people can use on the day. The dance school I mentioned offered a coupon which entitled all people who visited the display to a free lesson. A large proportion of the people who received the coupon took advantage of it and many of those ended up enrolling for complete courses. In fact this particular business ended up getting most of its business for the year from this one activity, which cost a few hundred dollars.

103 Make some smart promotional giveaways

If you sell a product that relies on people trying it before they buy it, give it away. We have a client who makes organic cheese and other dairy products. They are very good quality but they are expensive, about 30 per cent more expensive than competing mainstream products. This added expense is often a barrier to consumers buying the product because they don't realise how good it is.

The business owners tried a lot of alternative advertising including radio, television and newspaper but the one single most significant advertising success was when they held a tasting in a supermarket. The food is so good that normally with one try the average dairy food lover is hooked. The cost of giving away some product is negligible and the customers they get stay with them for a long time—in fact their loyalty to this brand is amazing.

I have another client who developed a range of organic coffee. As part of their production they arranged for small sampler bags to be produced as free giveaways. These were a big success because the risk for the consumer was taken out of the equation. They could try the coffee at no cost to them and if they liked it they could buy it the next time they visited the supermarket.

I am a firm believer in putting your wallet where your mouth is. Every business advertises they are the best at what they do— I have yet to see a business promote the fact they are mediocre but cheap so please give them a try (the principle of begging advertising). As consumers we have all been disappointed by products that haven't lived up to our expectations or the glossy brochure or the flash television commercial. Once burnt it will take a lot of convincing and a lot of advertising to get the customer back. If your product or service is as good as you believe it can be, give people a sample to try for themselves. This is how you can develop loyal customers who will stay with you for a long time, and they will tell everyone they know about your products or services.

This is a very accepted practice by a lot of larger companies and you will often see new product lines coming into supermarkets at really cheap prices. While they are not normally free they are very cheap, once again reducing the risk for the consumer to try the new product.

The same principle can be applied in service industries. For example, in my business we offer a 45-minute consultation free for new clients. During this time we will find out what they want and need and give them some ideas and recommendations. If they are happy they can come back as paying customers; if not, the risk to them is minimal because they have walked away with a free consultation and some ideas, and it has cost them nothing.

Put your money where your mouth is and you will be rewarded by attracting loyal customers.

104 Message on hold—the captive audience

Being put on hold while on the telephone is an everyday occurrence for most of us these days. If your customers get put on hold from time to time you might like to consider this as an opportunity to advertise your business to them.

Message on hold is simply a recorded message that enables specific pre-recorded messages to be played while the customers are on hold. It is relatively inexpensive and there are plenty of companies that offer this service.

Businesses should use message on hold to educate customers about what products and services their business offers. Regular customers may not be aware of the full range of services you offer and this is the perfect way to let them know.

To make the message on hold concept work it is important to change the messages regularly, otherwise it can start to sound like a broken record. I also recommend trying to keep the amount of time your customers are on hold to a bare minimum as time is precious and none of us like sitting on the end of a telephone waiting for service for too long.

Your messages for this need to be short sharp grabs or points rather than long drawn-out overly descriptive passages about how wonderful your business is.

105 Sell yourself at the movies

Advertising in cinemas has gone through ups and downs over the years. Cinema attendance numbers dropped with the introduction of videos but the crowds are back and they are bigger than ever. A visit to the cinema is high up on the list of recreational activities for most people who have a disposable income.

Typically cinema advertising consists of two main forms: slide style advertisements that show a businesses message with a voice over and the film style commercial. The film commercial is normally a business's television commercial aired at the cinema. Of course the screen is giant so the impact is just as giant. This type of advertising is relatively expensive but hard to miss. The slide advertisements don't move so the key to their success is to have a good voiceover and to make the slide grab the viewer's attention.

There is considerable debate over whether or not cinema advertising works. Do people remember the advertisements after being wowed by a movie? This is a good question and one that is dependent on the actual advertisement itself. I have had clients who have sworn by it and others who have felt the results were terrible.

Cinema advertising is a good way to reinforce your business's message and to increase awareness about the services and products your business offers, but as a stand-alone advertising tool I would consider other options first. The one exception to this is if your business is located close to the cinema and you can have a call to action that encourages the customer to visit the business after they have been to the cinema. This is ideal for food or entertainment-based businesses.

106 We all get dockets and most of us keep them

We are all familiar with the writing on the back of shopping dockets. Most large stores use this kind of advertising and more businesses are adopting the medium all the time. In fact, there are now lots of attractions, including movie cinemas, that have advertising on the back of their tickets. Another common one is car hire companies advertising on the back of airline boarding passes.

This type of advertising relies on large numbers of people receiving the advertising. What needs to be borne in mind is that most dockets are thrown in the bin. To really work the offer needs to be very good—it needs to catch attention. It also needs to be relevant and logical to the medium.

As always, think about your advertising before you commit to it. What is the message you are trying to get across to the person holding the docket or ticket and how will you make it stand out from the other advertisements in the same area? Bright colours, a clear picture and a very bold heading always help.

Think about the people who will be reading the advertisement. Put yourself in their shoes and think about how they will perceive your advertisement.

107   The good old business card

Never underestimate the advertising benefits of the business card. Just about everyone who owns a business has one and they are excellent tools for driving people to your business. Depending on the products and services your business offers, the business card can be used well to spread the word simply because you can hand them out to anyone you meet.

With business cards remember to include all your details, including your web address and perhaps list your products or services on the back of the card. Like all advertising, spend some time and energy planning your business cards—in fact in doing all of your stationery. I am constantly amazed that so many businesses have such poorly designed stationery. Potential customers will form a lot of perceptions about your business purely based on the design, layout and feel of your stationery.

I suggest you grab one of your business cards and letterheads this minute and have a good hard look at them. If they are less than impressive, pop down to the local graphic designer and get them to do some work on it for you. Having great stationery makes you proud to hand it out rather than feeling embarrassed if anyone sees it. Remember it costs as much to print really cheap, crappy stationery as it does to print really nice stationery.

108 Letterbox drop to success

Letterbox drops have been a part of the advertising stable for as long as letterboxes have been in existence. I don't think there are many people who don't get some form of advertising in their letterbox. Some people love it, some hate it. By doing a letterbox drop you can reach those people who love hearing about things through letterbox advertising.

Letterbox drops are relatively inexpensive. You normally pay a set price per thousand drops. The price can be anywhere between $50 and $100 as a general rule of thumb. This combined with the price of producing the flyer makes the whole exercise affordable for most businesses. You can also choose which suburbs you would like to have the flyers dropped to, making it a very specific target audience.

I have always recommended letterbox advertising for those businesses looking to attract new customers from a close-by geographical region. You can pick the surrounding suburbs of your business and organise your flyer to be dropped there. There are lots of companies that do the actual letterbox drops and if you have a look in a local telephone directory you will be able to find companies that will be able to help.

The real key to letterbox success is to make your flyer stand out. You will need to catch the potential customer's eye within seconds of being removed from the letterbox, otherwise your flyer may be on a one-way trip to the rubbish bin.

Stand out or be thrown out.

109 Take your message to the sky

This really is a bit of fun, but in its day skywriting was an advertising medium with a lot of impact. Sadly since the dawn of September 11, everyone is nervous about anything that flies and as a result skywriting has been virtually outlawed in lots of places.

The principle of skywriting is what I like. It is big and bold and there are no other advertising messages scattered around to distract the viewer. People love to watch the plane twisting and diving, all the time trying to figure out what it is going to write. To me this is the most pure form of advertising you can get. It is visual, it stands out from the crowd, it is unique, the audience loves to watch it and it is memorable.

By now I can almost hear you thinking, 'Yeah thanks, Andrew, for a goldmine advertising opportunity we can't use'. Well not entirely. I often use the skywriting principle when I am planning my advertising. I try to get it as close as I can to the skywriting concept in terms of uniqueness, standing out from the crowd, impact and innovation. If you apply the principles and the concept of the skywriter to all of your copy you will be surprised how much more effective it will be.

So even if you can't physically rent the plane, utilise the philosophy.

110 Flashing lights draw attention

You may laugh when you read this but I am a big believer in the benefits of flashing lights outside a business to attract customers or to attract attention to a business. Something as simple as this can have a huge bearing on whether people see the business.

I am often asked to troubleshoot roadside businesses that are having difficulties. They are in excellent locations but business is suffering. A step as simple as putting a row of flashing lights around a business sign can have a dramatic effect and I have seen it work time and time again.

The three simple keys to making this work are:

1. lots of lights (don't worry about the power bill)
2. changing the colour of the globes regularly
3. replacing blown globes regularly—nothing looks worse than half the lights not working.

Making your business stand out from the crowd is one of my key philosophies when it comes to success. Something as simple as putting a few flashing lights outside of your business can have surprising results.

Flags can work in a similar fashion. Large inflatable characters, music, smells or just about anything else that will make your business highly visible will work. My wife's mother and father used to own a delicatessen that sold roast chickens. They had the vent from the oven moved so that it came out over the footpath where there was a lot of passing pedestrian traffic. The smell attracted the crowds like bees to honey and they sold over 500 chickens every day.

The point I am making here is to think about your business from a number of different angles. Advertising has its mainstream versions but the whole concept of advertising is to get people into your business. I applaud anyone who can do this by thinking laterally about it.

Utilise all of the senses not just the most obvious one of sight and your advertising will definitely bring you attention.

111 Painted cows—advertising in the paddock

As an extension of tip #110 the concept of advertising on cows has become quite popular in recent times, particularly in the United Kingdom. Basically the company wanting to advertise puts its message on specially made covers worn by cows close to major freeways. The cows stay warm and dry and the company gets its advertising noticed in a unique and novel manner.

These sorts of opportunities abound and it is just a matter of being open to unusual ideas. I have a number of clients with quite unusual products. One has a barramundi farm. For those not aware of what a barramundi is, it is a much sought after fish that grows naturally in the tropical waters of northern Australia. Every day his farm has a pile of people dropping by to visit and have a look around. They take lots of photographs of the giant fish. Well, if you stop and think about how many people will see these pictures when they are developed, from all corners of the world, the most obvious thought will occur. Put a big sign around the main viewing chamber so every photograph will have the name of the barramundi farm in it. This has to be one of the cheapest forms of advertising available, yet it is surprising how rarely prime photographic locations are taken advantage of from an advertising point of view.

Now the barramundi farm has lots more people coming to visit because they saw the photographs and included the business as a must see attraction on their visit to Australia. Advertising doesn't get much better than that.

112 Send out media releases for free, instant advertising

I love free advertising and there are plenty of opportunities to get your business's name in the media if you go about it the right way. Writing a media release can be a daunting task for most people but you need to remember that the media is always keen to have newsworthy stories.

So what is a newsworthy topic for a media release? Well there are plenty. A few examples are listed below.

1. special events—new buildings, facilities or expansions; results of surveys; winning an award; business anniversaries; company mergers; joint ventures
2. employees—new management; key staff changes (promotions); staff member achievements or anniversaries; awards for employers; milestones for employees
3. financial—winning a major contract; plans for expansion; exporting products or ideas; achieving good financial results
4. technology—new technology or business practises; environmental announcements; new products or services
5. community—committing to sponsor a charity; committing to sponsor a sporting team; unusual happening, requests or results; special events the public are invited to attend.

These are just a few of the possible topics.

Writing a media release is relatively easy; as long as the basic information is included the media will contact you for more information if required. When writing a media release remember it is like writing an advertisement. First of all you need a good heading that gets attention. It is important it is newsworthy, not just a blatant promotional exercise. Every newspaper, radio station and television station gets hundreds of media releases a day so if yours doesn't stand out it will get thrown out.

Include all the important points in a few paragraphs. You need to answer the following questions in order to produce a successful media release:

- What has happened?
- Who does it affect?
- When will it/did it happen?
- How will it/did it happen?
- Why is it newsworthy?

Media releases should generally be only one page in length (a sample is attached in the blank forms section of this book). The font should be big enough to be read easily by the person receiving, especially if sent via fax, and it should always have a contact person and number at the end so the media know who to ask if they do want more information.

Try sending a media release when your business has a newsworthy event and you may be pleasantly surprised by the results and attention your business gets.

113 Are your advertising sales representatives asking the right questions?

Selling advertising space is a hard job. The industry is highly competitive and every time you turn around there is another type of advertising forum to compete with your own advertisements. Traditionally there were only five main types of advertising available—newspaper, magazine, television, radio and outdoor signage. Now there are hundreds to choose from and the advertising budgets of most companies have not increased to cover these new avenues. This basically means that selling advertising is about as competitive a job as you can get.

Good advertising sales representatives do very well. They get results for their clients, they get to know their clients and their businesses and they go out of their way to make advertising campaigns work. They ask the important questions such as:

1. What are you trying to achieve from this campaign?
2. Who is your target market?
3. What is the key selling point?
4. What is your budget?
5. Who is doing the production of the actual advertising piece?

There are a few more questions that can be asked for each particular medium but the ones above are the basics.

Our company works very closely with advertising sales representatives. We have worked with most of them for years and they know us, they know what we expect for our clients and they go out of their way to ensure we achieve the desired results. After all if we get good results for our clients they will keep coming back to us and in turn we will keep going back to buy more advertising space from the sales representatives.

Unfortunately not all advertising sales representatives are that good. Due to the difficulty of the business there is often a high turnover of staff. New staff are often not very knowledgeable about their product and they are under a lot of pressure to get results and to get these results fast. As a result they can take a short-term view towards selling advertising where it is all about meeting this month's budget rather than achieving solid results for their clients.

A good sales representative will ask the right questions. They will follow up during a campaign to see how it is going and they will follow up at the end of the campaign to ascertain the overall results. If it hasn't worked as well as anticipated they will work with you to try and understand why and will go out of their way to make the next campaign more effective.

If your advertising sales representative doesn't fit into this category, ask to be given another representative to service your account. Don't get caught up in personalities and likeable people—the number one priority is for your advertising to work. End of story.

114 What does an advertising agency do and cost?

Advertising agencies are set up to give businesses advice on where to advertise and how to advertise. This means the client normally gives the agency a brief explaining what the product or service they are trying to sell is, then the agency comes up with ideas on how to go about advertising it.

There are huge agencies and there are small one-person operations. Costs can vary dramatically and the industry as a whole has a reputation of being extravagant. Well, as an owner of an advertising agency, I can tell you those extravagant days are gone. Running an agency is a highly competitive business where clients expect results. If you don't deliver you won't have clients for very long.

Smart advertising agencies work with their clients with a clear understanding that the more successful the client the more successful the agency will be. The benefits of using an advertising agency are:

1. access to a creative pool of people to develop advertising concepts
2. the ability to get better rates when buying advertising due to the buying power of the agency
3. the advertising media will tend to be more willing to please an agency that books lots of media than a one-off client who books one campaign every blue moon
4. advertising agencies have skills most businesses do not have internally.

This aside, it is important to follow some simple steps when dealing with an advertising agency.

Firstly, the better the brief the better the outcome. This means making certain you really identify the specifics of what you want to achieve from the advertising campaign or, even more simply, how much product do you want to sell?

Secondly, if you have any questions or uncertainties about what the advertising agency is proposing make sure you talk to them about your concerns. This is much easier than everyone pointing the finger after a campaign has run. Building a relationship with your agency will save you money and time, and it will greatly increase your chances of advertising success. I have clients that I have been dealing with for many years. I know their businesses as well as I know mine. Advertising should work like clockwork and the level of communication between my business and my client's is excellent. In fact most of my clients have become very close personal friends. If their business goes through a rough time we will step in and help to get them back on track, normally at no cost.

The bottom line is work with your advertising agency and there are many benefits. But as always, it is your money and you must be fully aware of what you are spending, where you are spending it and why you are spending it.

A question I am often asked is, 'Can a small business use an advertising agency?' The answer is, yes. There are lots of small advertising agencies that specialise in dealing with small- to medium-sized businesses. The prices they charge vary considerably from agency to agency. Some agencies like to work on a flat hourly rate, others work on a combination of commission (from any advertising they book on behalf of the client) and an hourly rate. The rates and conditions are normally discussed in a preliminary meeting, which is free. I believe you get what you pay for but if an agency is any good they will have a list of happy customers they will welcome you to call to verify their abilities. If they don't, ask yourself why not?

115 Use your business foyer to advertise your business

A lot of money is spent on mainstream advertising but often little thought is put into maximising the benefits of attracting customers by advertising to them once they arrive at your business. We often make the big assumption that our customers know as much about our business as we do. We assume they know all of our products and the reasons why they should spend their money in our business. If you do ask a few questions you will soon realise most customers know very little about your business.

I often recommend to my clients to actually ask a few customers to list the products and services they think the business offers. It is very rare for the level of customer knowledge about the business's products and services to be high, apart from the products or services they buy on a regular basis. For this reason all businesses should use their foyers or reception areas to tell their customers about the complete range of their products and services.

This might be in the form of a simple brochure rack or a television with a corporate video on a loop. Signs can help, as can simple flyers given to customers whenever they make a purchase. Customers like to know about the businesses they deal with and I have always found them to be receptive to this form of advertising.

Like all forms of advertising you need to change your foyer displays on a regular basis as customers (especially frequent ones) can become blind to the same message if they see it time and time again. Move things around, change the video, change the promotional material and most of all, take some time once a month to review this valuable area to make sure you are using your foyer or reception area to the maximum. Of course if you don't have a reception area or a foyer the same principles can easily apply to a workshop, retail shop, office or just about any other workplace area—wherever customers visit.

If you can, take a few moments right now to look around

the front of your workplace. Are you promoting your business as well as you could? Are there areas where you could put your promotional material on display, perhaps a few certificates or even letters from customers, or even just have a big sign on the wall detailing exactly what it is you do?

116 Remember every city is different

A common mistake with advertising is the assumption that all people are the same. An extension of this is assuming all cities are the same. As an example, I live in a very warm, tropical city. We don't really have a winter and for most of the year shorts and t-shirts are more than adequate to keep you protected from the elements. But without fail, large national advertisers promote the sale of heaters in the winter months. I don't know any one of my friends who actually owns a heater and we often chuckle when these advertisements come on television.

Likewise, travel companies advertise tropical holidays which feature palm fringed beaches and crystal clear waters. Anyone living in the tropics has more than enough of both. In fact, they tend to look for holidays in cool climates just for the change.

The point I am making is that if you are advertising across more than one city make sure you do your homework and ensure you have got things right. Don't waste your money advertising a product which will have very limited appeal to the majority of people in the city where you are advertising.

It is easy to just book your advertising to cover a few cities or states but if it is ineffectual why bother? Do your research and try to find out about the areas where you plan to advertise to make sure you are going to send the right message and sell the right product.

117 The advertising brainstorm—a powerful weapon

The ideas that can be collected from having a round table discussion with a group of like-minded and positive people is really quite impressive. Having an advertising brainstorm could be one way to gather together some new ideas to promote your business.

The concept of the advertising brainstorm is to get your group to take turns in discussing how you advertise your individual business and what you have found to work well and what you have found to be less successful (or downright dismal). It is also an opportunity to ask for input from the other participants on what their thoughts are about your advertising.

To have a successful brainstorm it is important everyone involved is there to give constructive input and to relate their own experiences. To be this open it is likely you will only have an advertising brainstorm with people who you know reasonably well and people you feel comfortable with. Having one person chair or run the meeting is a way to ensure it progresses in a productive manner and that everyone has the opportunity to voice their opinions and to get feedback from the other participants. Have an agenda set or a time frame to be adhered to, otherwise some participants may miss out.

Forming a small club that meets on a regular basis to discuss advertising and other issues is always a positive step in the right direction.

118 Advertise your brand

Branding is an advertising term that gets thrown around a lot. Most businesses are not aware of what their actual brand is or even that they have a brand. It is a lot more than just the name of a specific product but that is how brands are most well known.

I believe your brand is the image you portray. Your company name evokes an emotional feeling and hopefully a good feeling from existing and potential customers. One example that comes to mind is Volvo—you immediately have the perception of a safe, solid motor vehicle because that is the way Volvo have developed their brand.

All businesses can promote themselves as a brand. Coca-Cola promotes itself as the catalyst for having a good time—drink Coke and you will have lots of fun. Of course this isn't necessarily true but it is the way the brand has been developed with smart advertising over many years.

Banks promote themselves as safe and secure, which makes sense because that's where we want our money to be—somewhere safe and secure. Food businesses tend to promote their brand from a wholesome point of view, making us feel good about what we will be eating. Your brand is your business and the image it portrays to potential customers. What emotions does your business conjure?

The first part of promoting your brand is to decide exactly what feelings you want to be associated with your business and then develop your advertising to encourage these feelings.

119 Every letter, invoice, envelope, email and fax has advertising potential

One of the best ways to advertise your business, which is often overlooked, is your office stationery. Most businesses send out a lot of letters, bills and faxes. I always suggest you take full advantage of this correspondence by advertising your services or products on your stationery. How many potential customers handle your correspondence—from the postman to the CEO of a company you may be sending a letter to, and a lot of people in between?

Limit your advertising message to one or two lines and make it stand out on your correspondence. Odds on the person you are sending the information to is already a customer so they will generally know a certain amount about your business but you could use this opportunity to tell them about a new product or service you now offer.

One other form of office stationery that is often forgotten is your email signature. This is where a message automatically appears at the end of any emails you send. The way you set this up varies slightly for each Internet browser and a quick visit to the help section will normally have you on the way to setting up your email signature in a matter of minutes. This signature can be changed regularly and as we all start sending more and more emails, it is an excellent way to advertise certain aspects of your business. By the way, you can also put a link to your websites in the same area, which makes it easy for people reading your emails to visit your site.

Like all advertising, put some thought into what you want to achieve from putting an advertising message on your office correspondence and stationery and then plan it accordingly.

120 Research often—attack magazines and newspapers with scissors

In my first book, *101 Ways to Market Your Business*, and this one, I discuss the idea of establishing a marketing ideas box. Basically this is a library of all the clever marketing and advertising ideas you can collect over many years. For me, this is my most prized possession simply because of the wealth of information it contains (this reminds me that I need to get a life).

I am always recommending to my clients and my readers to start their own ideas box. Take to magazines, newspapers, brochures and your morning mail with scissors. If you find a promotional piece that catches your attention and makes you stop and read it, then the odds are pretty good there is something smart in this particular advertisement. You may be able to adapt the idea or the concept and use it to advertise your own business.

To really succeed with advertising you need to study it. You need to ask questions and to be objective about the advertising that comes across your desk. If you are constantly looking for and have an open mind to new ideas you will soon see you are surrounded by them. There are a lot of very good advertising people out there who are exceptionally talented when it comes to being creative. If your business can benefit from this creative talent why not use it.

So whip out today, grab yourself a strong box and start collecting. Next time you are planning to advertise, pull out the box and look for some creative inspiration from the information it contains.

121 Conduct your own market research to avoid wasting money

What is the point of spending money on advertising if you can't work out whether or not it is working? At the beginning of this book I mentioned a fabulous quotation commonly used when discussing advertising: 'Half of my advertising works and half of it doesn't. The problem I have is figuring out which half is which.'

Using market research to determine the effectiveness of your advertising is not as complicated as most people imagine. The best way to measure your advertising effectiveness is to get into the habit of asking people how they heard about your business. Many modern cash registers can have this question programmed into them so the sales assistant has to ask you this question before the sales can be concluded. Another way is to have a simple form and pencil beside the telephone or on the front counter where a box can be ticked when this question is asked. Customers are usually more than happy to answer this question and I actually believe they like it because it shows the business is thinking about what it is doing. Smart businesses know where their customers come from.

The options to consider when asking this question depend on where you currently advertise but the following list should cover most options.

How did you find out about this business?

On television	❏
On the radio	❏
In the newspaper (which one?)	❏
A friend told me about the business	❏
Driving or walking past	❏
An outdoor billboard or sign	❏
On the Internet	❏
In a magazine (which one?)	❏

Recommended by another business   ❏
Other (please specify) _____

Over time you will collect a lot of valuable information and the source where most people have heard about your business will soon become clear.

A word of warning though—when people recall your advertising they will tend to remember the one that most impacted on them or the advertising they saw most recently. Not the one that first brought their attention to you. Use the information you collect as a guide and look for the most common responses. Once you have this information, you come to think about your advertising in a different light. By being informed you will greatly reduce the chances of wasting your advertising spend.

Notes

Advertising action list

Things to do   **Completed**

1. _____   _____

2. _____   _____

3. _____   _____

4. _____   _____

5. _____   _____

6. _____   _____

7. _____   _____

8. _____   _____

9. _____   _____

10. _____   _____

A final word from the author

Advertising does work. The key to its effectiveness is to put a lot of thought into the planning of your advertising to make sure it is going to be as effective as possible. Remember, advertising is a business tool that can be used to attract more customers and ultimately make your business more profitable. Plan your advertising well, be prepared to try new ideas and work at making your advertising stand out from the crowd and you will be well on the way to success.

Anyone can advertise their business but very few people advertise their business effectively. I hope this book has given you a clearer understanding of the advertising process and that the tips and suggestions I have recommended will enable you to build a profitable and successful business.

Andrew Griffiths
www.andrewgriffiths.com.au
www.themarketingprofessionals.com.au

Glossary of advertising terms

Understanding the jargon

The advertising industry works with its own language, which very few people outside of the industry understand (and in fact many within the industry don't understand either). Don't get trapped by the jargon. You do need to understand some of it but don't be baffled by it. Advertising sales representatives often throw terms around that mean nothing to the poor unsuspecting customer—it can be a ploy on their part. If you don't know what they are talking about ask them. Most people don't have a clue so there is no reason to feel bad.

I have included on the following pages most of the common terms and jargon used across the various media to help you feel a little more sure of yourself. There are lots more that are quite specific to the circumstance and if you want a greater understanding of these go online and search under the keyword 'advertising jargon'. A few interesting sites may come up. I have specifically tried to avoid using jargon in this book but in some areas it is virtually impossible. For those readers with a good knowledge of the jargon I was in no way trying to be condescending—simply uncomplicated.

Term	Media most often used in	Meaning
Advertorial	All media	An advertisement that appears to be a news story.
Brief	All media	This is like a plan for your advertising. It explains what you would like to be achieved from the campaign, the amount of money you intend to spend on the campaign and the time frame the campaign would adhere to. This is normally given to your advertising agency or the advertising sales representative selling you advertising.
Circulation	Newspapers and magazines	The number of publications sold.
Column space	Newspapers and magazines	Generally used to describe the size of an advertisement. All newspaper pages are split into columns; the number varies as does the width. Advertising space tends to be measured by the number of columns, by the centimetres or inches. The number of columns tells you how wide the advertisement will be and the number of centimetres or inches tells you how high the advertisement will be.
Copy	All media	This is the text to form the basis of the advertisement or the commercial. Copy is normally supplied to the organisation producing the material. If asked

		to supply copy for editorial consideration, supply up to 500 words that can be culled down according to the length of the article.
Deadline	All media	The latest time to submit material for advertising.
Demographic	All media	A general description used to determine the type of people you want to see your advertisements (age group, employment, location etc.).
Early right hand	Newspapers and magazines	Describes the prime advertising pages—close to the front and on a right-hand page.
Impacts	Television	The total number of people who have seen the campaign.
Flighting	All media	Ongoing advertising that runs automatically.
Frequency	Television and radio	The average number of times viewers were exposed to the commercial.
Key number	Television and radio	A unique number used to identify your commercials. Even slight changes to an advertisement require the issuing of a new key number.
Layout	Newspapers and magazines	The design of an advertisement.
Live read	Radio	Commercial read live by an announcer.
Loading	All media	Extra cost paid for prime position of advertisements or commercials.

Masthead	Newspapers and magazines	Generally refers to the top of the front page of a newspaper or magazine. Can also refer to an advertisement that runs across a page in a similar format.
Position	Newspapers and magazines	Where the advertisement appears in the publication.
Production	All media	Generally refers to the production of your advertisement or commercial.
Ratings	Television and radio	The number of people of various age groups that view or listen to a particular programme or time slot.
Reach	Television and radio	The number of people in your targeted audience who had at least one opportunity to see/hear your campaign.
Run of station	Television and radio	Commercials aired at non-specific times on television or radio (generally during lower rating time slots).
Schedule	Television and radio	A detailed plan showing the days and times your commercials will be aired. It is supplied by the station, normally in the form of a proposal.
Storyboards	Television	Rough sketches showing the concept of a television commercial. Storyboards are used to plan television commercials.
TRP (or TARP)	Television	TARP (Target Audience Rating Point) is a way of measuring

how many people could potentially see a particular commercial based on the schedule provided by the station. It provides a means of comparing schedules between television stations.

For example, if the ABC Corporation decided that its market was men aged 18–45 and it aired commercials at 9 p.m. on a particular station where 20 per cent of the viewing audience fitted into this demographic, the commercial has a TARP of 20. Each time the commercial is aired the TARP figure is accumulated so the commercial might acquire a total of 200 for the week. Generally, the higher the TARP the more impact the campaign will have.

Voiceover	Television	The sound track for a television commercial.

Smart advertising words and phrases

One of the biggest stumbling blocks for many people planning advertising is what words and phrases to use. For this reason I have included this quick reference to help you find the right kinds of words and phrases to give your advertisements extra punch. All you need to do is fill in your product/service names on the dotted line where appropriate to gauge how well it will work for you. Hopefully, these words and phrases will act as a springboard to other ideas you may have. The topics included here are:

1. Words and phrases to use as headings
2. Opening with a question
3. Opening with a statement
4. Opening with a challenge
5. Other grabbers
6. Persuading the reader
7. Words to help the customer make the decision now
8. Encouraging the customer to contact the business right now (the call to action)
9. Are you stuck for the right word to evoke a specific emotion?

1. Words and phrases to use as headings

A little .... can go a long way

A major breakthrough in ....

A .... from the word 'go'

A .... for all seasons

Always go to an expert ....

Amazing medical breakthrough!

An investment in your future

Announcing the first ....

At ...., you're number 1

Built to last

Can you afford not to?

Celebrate with ....

Check us out

Don't gamble with ....

Don't get stuck with ....

Don't wait for success to come to you!

Everything you always wanted to know about ....

Finally, there's a better way to ....

Food for thought

For the finest in ...., look to ....

For those special people in your life

For those special times

Get comfortable with ....

Get hooked on ....

Go all the way!

Go with a winner

How do you turn a .... into a ....?

How our .... stacks up

In a class by itself

Instant ....

It takes talent and we've got it

It's easy to see ....

It's easy to spot the winners

It's elementary ....

It's time for ....
Meet the newest addition to our family
Not just another ....
Nothing sells like a ....
Nothing's built like a ....
Now, more than ever, you need ....
Only .... gives you ....
Say, 'Yes!' to ....
Seeing is believing
So easy a child can do it
Some straight talk about ....
State-of-the-art ....
Success starts with ....
Switch to ....
Take a chance with ....
Take a minute to ....
Taste the difference!
The answer to your prayers
The best kept secret in ....
The dependables
The fun begins with ....
The legend lives
The only way to ....
The price cutters
The smart choice
The .... that works as hard as you do
The .... guys
The .... pledge
The .... advantage
The .... edge
The .... experts
The ....'s best friend
There's no substitute for ....
They don't call us .... for nothing
Train for the future

Turn your life around!
We don't cut corners
Who says you can't win 'em all?
Why your first .... should be a ....
What makes us different?
You'll swear by us—not at us!
Your partner in ....
Your shortcut to ....
...............—for those who insist on the best
.... is our business
.... in your pocket
.... where you want it, when you want it
.... doesn't have to be expensive
.... fever!
.... is our middle name
.... means business
.... reasons why you should ....
.... spoken here!

2. **Opening with a question**
Are you curious about ....?
Are you drowning in a sea of ....?
Are you interested in ....?
Are you intrigued by ....?
Are you ready for ....?
Are you still ....?
Confused about which .... to buy?
Could you use an extra $............... each month?
Did you ever ask yourself ....?
Did you know that ....?
Do you want a better job?
Do you want to stretch your purchasing power?
Don't you need ....?
Don't you wish ....?
Have you ever stayed awake at night thinking about
...............?

Have you ever thought about ....?
How can you cut the high cost of ....?
How many times have you said to yourself, ...?
How much is your company spending on ....?
How secure is your job?
Isn't it time you ....?
Tired of empty promises from ....?
Tired of the same old ....?
Want to keep in touch with ....?
Want to stay abreast of ....?
What would you say if we offered to help you ....?
What's the best investment you could make?
What's the most effective way to ....?
What's the most profitable ....?
What's the safest ....?
Who can put a price on ....?
Who could say no to ....?
Why pay full price for .... when you can buy for less at ....?
Why postpone your future in ....?
Why sacrifice .... for ....?
Why should you use .... when you can ....?
Why trade a .... for a ....?
Will you be ready for the ....?
Will you risk just $1.00 to ....?
Wouldn't you like to ....?

3. Opening with a statement

Believe it or not, ...
Every once in a while you come across a ....
that ....
For under $............... you can ....
In the 10 seconds it took you to read this far, ...
In today's competitive marketplace, ...
In today's uncertain economy, ...

It isn't enough to be ....
It's a fact of life that ....
It's hard enough to .... without having to worry about ....
It's never too early to ....
It's never too late to ....
It's no secret that ....
It's not every day that ....
Just a note to tell you about ....
Let us sell you on ....
Let's be honest ....
Let's face it ....
Now you can ....
Now, the real truth about ....
The results are in ....
Think about ....
Today, more than ever, ...
We live in an increasingly complex society ....
We'll change your mind about ....
We've got the solution to your ....
Within 30 days from today, you could be ....
You can organise a successful ....
You're in for a pleasant surprise.
You're the kind of person who ....
You've probably noticed that ....
.... may determine the future of your business.
.... often spells the difference between failure and success.

4. Opening with a challenge
Be a winner!
Be your own .... [mechanic, plumber etc.]!
Capture the ....
Cross the threshold ....
Delve into the ....

Discover the ....
Do something extraordinary!
Don't let .... keep you from getting ahead.
Encounter the ....
Enjoy the ....
Experience the ....
Explore the ....
If you sincerely want to ....
If you think you're good enough ....
If you're seriously interested in ....
Join the small handful of people who ....
Join the ....
Just wait until you ....
Learn about the ....
Let your imagination soar!
Make time for ....
Match wits with ....
Match yourself against ....
Meet the ....
Relive the ....
Return to the ....
Sample the ....
Say, 'Yes' to ....
Take a giant step ....
Visit the ....
.... like a professional!

5. **Other grabbers**
   As seen on TV.
   At last!
   Attention!
   By popular demand.
   Check these super features!
   Don't miss out.
   Exclusive!

Fact: ....
For a limited time only.
Forget everything you've heard about ....
Good news!
Grand opening!
Here's what you get: ....
Hurry in for these ....
Important!
It's true!
Limited numbers.
Major breakthrough!
New low price!
New!
No problem!
Now for the first time ....
Now you too can ....
Our loss is your gain!
Satisfaction guaranteed or your money back.
Sneak preview!
Something to cheer about!
The first and only ....
The first ....
The only ....
This is your last chance to ....
Treat yourself to a ....
Urgent!
Valuable document enclosed!
You bet!
.... reasons why you should buy ....

6. Persuading the reader
And it is totally tax deductable.
A rewarding .... awaits you.
All this can be yours.
Can you think of any reason not to send for your ....?

Does all this sound too good to be true?

Frankly, I can't understand why everybody doesn't take advantage of this offer.

If you'd like to become part of today's ...., there's no better way to start than ....

If you're like most people, you probably ....

If you've been waiting for the right ...., you don't have to wait any longer.

If .... is your passion, then you'll appreciate ....

Imagine being able to get a .... for only $...............!

In short, you've got nothing to lose.

In the last analysis, all that matters is ....

It's no wonder that we're the number one choice ....

Once you try us, you'll want to stay with us.

Our supply is limited.

Put your .... to the test.

Remember, time is running out.

Seeing is believing.

Take advantage of this special offer.

Take as many as you wish—or none at all!

That's all it takes to ....

There's just one conclusion: ....

Think of what you have to look forward to!

This is the opportunity you've been waiting for.

Try to imagine the alternative.

We need you .... you need us!

We stand behind our claims.

We think you'll agree ....

We think you'll find that ....

We're ready to prove everything we claim.

We're sure to have the perfect .... for you.

What have you got to lose?

When every dollar counts, it's good to know that ....

Why settle for .... when you can have ....?
You can see for yourself that ....
You can't lose.
You won't be disappointed.
You'll be glad you did.
You'll receive all these benefits: ....
You'll still be able to do it your way—only better!
You'll want to add it to your personal collection.
You'll wonder how you ever managed without it.
You'll wonder why you waited.
You've waited long enough.
.... and that's a promise!

7. **Words to help the customer make the decision now**
   Act now!
   Are you convinced yet?
   But do it now!
   But don't just take our word for it—find out for yourself!
   Check it out.
   Decide for yourself!
   Do it today!
   Don't delay!
   Don't hesitate!
   Don't miss out!
   Don't miss this opportunity!
   Don't wait any longer!
   Interested?
   Intrigued?
   It's a winning decision to make.
   It's time to make your choice.
   It's up to you.
   Make this the turning point of your life.
   Now is the best time!
   Now it's time for you to decide.

Order now while there's still time.
Put our ideas to work!
Rather than simply reading about it, why don't you
................?
Reserve your space today!
Say, 'Yes' to ....
See for yourself.
So, what are you waiting for?
Take this important first step.
There is no time like the present.
This is your moment!
Time's running out!
We need you.
We're expecting you.
Why wait another day?
You be the judge.
You can do it!
You'll just have to experience it for yourself.
You've got an important decision to make.
You've waited long enough.

8. **Encouraging the customer to contact the business right now (the call to action)**
A visit to our website is the first step.
An order form is enclosed for your convenience.
Call our free call number.
Call us this week to schedule an appointment.
Call us today—we're in the book.
Come in and introduce yourself!
Come in and let us show you around.
Don't take our word for it, ask your friends.
For a free demonstration call ....
For even faster service, call ....
For more details call your ....
Get all the facts.

Hurry in for a demonstration.
I can't wait to hear from you.
In a hurry? Call ....
It really is the logical choice to make.
Join thousands of other satisfied customers today.
Just drop us a letter.
Just fill out the convenient order form.
Just reach for your phone.
Let us visit you at your convenience.
Mail this convenient coupon today!
Mail your order today!
Our customer service team is waiting for your call.
Our representative will call you at your convenience.
Please don't hesitate to call us.
Please return it to me at your earliest convenience.
Send for our colourful catalogue.
Send for our free catalogue.
Send in your application today!
The solution is just a phone call away.
We look forward to hearing from you.
We'll be glad to show you around.
We're looking forward to seeing you.
We're waiting for your call.
What have you got to lose by calling today?
What are you waiting for? Call right now!
Why not drop in and say hello today?
Why not give us a call and find out more?
Write for your free copy of our brochure.

9. **Are you stuck for the right word to evoke a specific emotion?**

   There are plenty to choose from but the ones listed here may help to get you started. All of the words listed evoke a feeling or emotion and they can be used in advertising copy to portray that emotion to the reader.

Alluring	Genuine	Soothing
Amazing	Gigantic	Spectacular
Beautiful	Glorious	Staggering
Bold	Gripping	Strength
Breathtaking	Guaranteed	Striking
Captivating	Handy	Stunning
Casual	Imaginative	Substantial
Challenging	Immense	Superb
Classic	Innovative	Superior
Colossal	Inviting	Sweeping
Compelling	Irresistible	Tangled
Completely	Lethal	Temptation
Creative	Monumental	Tender
Crucial	Overwhelming	Terrific
Deadly	Passionate	Threatening
Delightful	Powerful	Tough
Dramatic	Precious	Towering
Dynamic	Professional	Tranquil
Electrifying	Proven	Tremendous
Elegant	Rare	Trusted
Energy	Real	Unforgettable
Enlightening	Refined	Unified
Essential	Reliable	Vibrant
Excellence	Remarkable	Vital
Experienced	Rugged	Wholesome
Exquisite	Seductive	Wild
Fascinating	Serene	Wow
Forceful	Shocking	
Futuristic	Sizzling	

Blank forms and advertising checklists

The following forms have been designed to help you to plan your advertising. They can be adapted for use in your own business. Having something as simple as a checklist for preparing advertisements can make advertising your business much easier and much more effective. Included are:

1. Advertising campaign plan
2. Briefing form to give to media sales representative
3. Printed advertisement checklist
4. Radio commercial checklist
5. Television commercial checklist
6. Sample media release
7. A simple form for monitoring your advertising

1. Advertising campaign plan

The following campaign plan is designed as a one-page summary for a specific advertising campaign. Each piece of advertising you do could have its own plan according to its needs.

Campaign title: ....

Person in charge: ....

Start date: ....

Finish date: ....

Campaign overview: ....

....

....

Campaign objectives: ....

....

....

Medium	Budget	Production	Total
Newspaper	....	....	....
Magazine	....	....	....
Radio	....	....	....
Television	....	....	....
Outdoor signs	....	....	....
Internet	....	....	....
Total campaign costs	....	....	....

Method for monitoring results ....

....

....

Comments ....

....

....

2. Briefing form to give to media sales representative

This form can be used as a brief to obtain prices for advertising from your media sales representative.

Media company: ....

Sales executive: ....

Company: ....

Campaign title: ....

Contact person: ....

Start date: ....

Finish date: ....

Campaign overview: ....

....

....

Campaign objectives: ....

....

....

Target market: ....

....

Advertising budget: ....

....

Final date for
  submission: ....

Other media supplying
  quotations: ....

....

....

Comments: ....

....

....

---

continues

Medium	Budget	Production	Total
Newspaper	....	....	....
Magazine	....	....	....
Radio	....	....	....
Television	....	....	....
Outdoor signs	....	....	....
Internet	....	....	....
Total campaign costs	....	....	....

Method for monitoring results ....

....

....

Comments ....

....

....

3. Printed advertisement checklist

The following checklist can be used when planning your printed advertisements.

What are we trying to sell? ....
....

Why should customers buy the product? ....
....
....

Publication: ....
Material due by: ....
Size : ....
Style: B&W   Spot colour   Full colour
Position in the publication: ....

Checklist

Strong bold heading   ❏
Copy is logical and motivational   ❏
All contact details included   ❏
Final call to action   ❏
Advertisement checked for mistakes   ❏
Advertisement double checked for mistakes   ❏
Supplied to publication by due date   ❏
Supplied by whom and in what format: ....
....

Checked that advertisement ran   ❏

Results: ....
....

Comments: ....
....

4. Radio commercial checklist

The following checklist can be used to develop a radio commercial to promote your business.

What are we trying to sell? ....

....

Why should customers buy the product? ....

....

Station/s to be used: ....
Material due by: ....
Length of commercial: 15 sec   30 sec   Other
Style: Recorded   Live read

Checklist

Distinctive sound to catch attention   ❏
Follows a logical sequence   ❏
Does commercial stand out   ❏
Main message repeated   ❏
Call to action included   ❏
Commercial tested   ❏
Supplied to radio station by due date   ❏
Supplied by whom and in what format: ....

....

Checked that commercials aired   ❏

Results: ....

....

Comments: ....

....

....

---

5. Television commercial checklist

What are we trying to sell? ....
....
....
Why should customers buy the product? ....
....
....

Station/s to be used: ....
Material due by: ....
Length of commercial: 15 sec   30 sec   45 sec   60 sec

Checklist

Attention grabber at beginning ☐
Commercial flows in a logical manner ☐
Style for voiceover decided ☐
Main message repeated ☐
Does commercial stand out? ☐
Call to action included ☐
Commercial tested ☐
Supplied to television station by due date ☐
Supplied by whom and in what format: ....
....
Checked that commercials aired ☐

Results: ....
....

Comments: ....
....
....

6. Sample media release

28th June 2002

'FAMILIES WELCOMED'

For immediate release—CAIRNS, NORTH QUEENSLAND

Long established and well known Port Douglas restaurant, Mango Jam, was awarded the title of Best Family Establishment in the recent Queensland, Far North Queensland Restaurant and Catering Association Awards. This is a significant achievement for an individual restaurant amongst a sea of formatted restaurants targeting the family market.

Owner John Hill explained, 'We have worked very actively at encouraging families to dine at Mango Jam. Port Douglas attracts a lot of families, tourists and local residents alike and many restaurants don't really cater for these families. As a result we realised there was niche in the market and we developed a number of innovative concepts that have proven very popular with children, including a special kids' menu that doubles as an activities board and a sun visor, colouring-in books, activity centre and special desserts.' Mango Jam is also one of the most successful restaurants in Queensland with a very modern and proactive approach to marketing and a comprehensive quality control system in place, resulting in the restaurant attracting tens of thousands of families every year.

Restaurant Manager, Mr David Robertson, stated, 'The award means a lot to all of us. We have a dedicated team working in the restaurant and we are proud of the food we produce and the service we offer. To be recognised as the leading family restaurant in North Queensland helps to reinforce our belief that we are on the right track and it means our hard work is paying off.'

For more information please contact: John Hill, owner, 4099 4611 or David Robertson, manager, 4099 4611— Mango Jam Restaurant, 24 Macrossan St, Port Douglas, www.mango jam.com.au

7. A simple form for monitoring your advertising

This can be kept by the telephone or on the front counter of your business. All it requires is a simple tick in the right box. The ticks can be tallied up at the end of each week or month and you should end up with accurate figures on where your business comes from and what advertising is working for you.

Where did our customers hear about us?	Total
Television advertising ☐☐☐☐☐☐☐☐	....
Radio advertising ☐☐☐☐☐☐☐☐	....
The Yellow Pages ☐☐☐☐☐☐☐☐	....
The newspaper ☐☐☐☐☐☐☐☐	....
Letterbox drop ☐☐☐☐☐☐☐☐	....
The Internet ☐☐☐☐☐☐☐☐	....
Outdoor billboard ☐☐☐☐☐☐☐☐	....
Driving past the business ☐☐☐☐☐☐☐☐	....
Recommended by a friend ☐☐☐☐☐☐☐☐	....
Shopped here before ☐☐☐☐☐☐☐☐	....

Other (state what other is if known) ....
....

Top five for this week	Top five from last week
1.	1. ....
2.	2. ....
3.	3. ....
4.	4. ....
5.	5. ....

Recommended reading

Bayan, Richard, 1984, *Words that Sell*, Contemporary Books, Chicago.

Caples, John, 1997, *Tested Advertising Methods (Fifth Edition)*, Prentice Hall, New Jersey.

Denton, Andrew, 2000, *How to Write and Pitch Your Press Release*, Prentice Hall, Sydney.

Griffiths, A., 2000, *101 Ways to Market Your Business*, Allen & Unwin, Sydney.

Griffiths, A., 2002, *101 Survival Tips for Your Business*, Allen & Unwin, Sydney.

Griffiths, A., 2002, *101 Ways to Really Satisfy Your Customers*, Allen & Unwin, Sydney.

Sutherland, M., 2000, *Advertising and the Mind of the Consumer*, Allen & Unwin, Sydney.

Switzer, P., 2002, *350 Ways to Grow Your Small Business*, Harper Collins, Sydney.

Other books available in the 101 series

101 Ways to Market Your Business—**Andrew Griffiths**
If you are looking for a collection of tried and tested, simple and cost effective marketing ideas this is the book for you. The ideas recommended can be implemented immediately and they will definitely increase income for your business. This book became an international best seller within months of being released. It is available around the world and it has even been translated into Chinese.

101 Survival Tips for Your Business—**Andrew Griffiths**
Everyone makes mistakes in business—it is simply a fact of business life. Now a book has been written based on the experience of many successful business owners and operators and it can identify the most common mistakes and, best of all, show you how to avoid making the same mistakes yourself. This book is a veritable gold mine of information that can save you a lot of money and make your business more successful in a shorter period of time.

101 Ways to Really Satisfy Your Customers—**Andrew Griffiths**
The level of customer service that your business offers will make all the difference between overwhelming success and struggling mediocrity in your business life. This book will identify the most

common customer service faults and how to avoid them. It will also give you over a hundred inspirational ideas on how to stand out from the crowd by offering better customer service than your competitors.

About Andrew Griffiths

Andrew Griffiths is a professional marketing and public relations consultant. He has three other books published, *101 Ways to Market Your Business, 101 Survival Tips for Your Business* and *101 Ways to Really Satisfy Your Customers*, all of which have become international best sellers. They are all now available in over 30 countries around the world and have been translated into Chinese and are published in India.

Andrew is the Director of an Australian company called The Marketing Professionals, offering innovative marketing and public relations advice. In his career Andrew has owned and operated a number of businesses including a commercial diving operation, a travel company, an outdoor advertising business and a publishing business. He has worked as a dive instructor and commercial diver, door-to-door encyclopaedia salesman, gold prospector, international sales manager and gardener. He lives in Cairns, Australia, the gateway to The Great Barrier Reef.

Andrew is passionate about small business and has enormous drive to inspire people to achieve their goals. He has a realistic and experience based view on how to run and market a business. Andrew is sought out as a marketing and public relations trouble-shooter and is an accomplished public speaker.

To find out more about Andrew Griffiths and The Marketing Professionals visit www.andrewgriffiths.com.au or www.the marketingprofessionals.com.au.

To find out more about Cairns, Australia or The Great Barrier Reef visit www.cairnsconnect.com.